MIRACLES
AND
MEMORIES

MIRACLES
AND
MEMORIES

ROGER DEAN GUDEMAN

CITI OF
BOOKS

CITIOFBOOKS, INC.
3736 Eubank NE Suite A1
Albuquerque, NM 871113579
www.citiofbooks.com
Hotline: 1 (877) 3892759
Fax: 1 (505) 9307244

Ordering Information:

Quantity sales. Special discounts are available on quantity purchases by corporations, associations, and others. For details, contact the publisher at the address above.

Printed in the United States of America.

ISBN13:   Softcover   979-8-89391-032-2

Library of Congress Control Number: 2024906324

TABLE OF CONTENTS

FOREWORD

Each of these stories is a testimony to the miracles that God performs daily in each of our lives and thoughts. Although they are not true stories of actual happenings, they are all miracles of actual happenings in our minds, which lead to so many great memories in our lives. Every day we spend here on earth is a miracle, and the longer we spend here leads to more miracles and more memories. Remember, we don't find God, He finds us and every memory we have of this is a miracle in itself.

DEDICATION

These stories are dedicated to the memory of my parents, who gave me most of the memories that started my dreams. There is a story about each of them, my thoughts as to their last day on earth, and they are the inspiration for so many more of the stories. To my parents; thanks for the miracles, the memories, and the blessed, God-fearing lives that you inspired. I still love you and miss you, and look forward to meeting you again in that great glorious final day, when we shall all be taken home with the Lord, to stand before Him brand-new, pure and perfect.

ACKNOWLEDGMENTS

On a Friday afternoon at three o'clock, on what has become known as "Good Friday," hanging on my cross, bearing my sins and the sins of the world, in the dark, alone, abandoned by all men, forsaken by His own father, the Almighty Heavenly Father, suffering the righteous wrath of God against me, Jesus died my death and paid my debt completely, freeing me completely from my sins.

SYNOPSIS

A short while back a friend mentioned to me that he didn't know I was a writer. I told him that I had been a professional truck-driver since 1970 when I was 19 years old and I am not a writer. I am a story-teller. I write the stories I am given, and I appreciate you reading my stories and I hope a few of them hit you where you live and that they may draw you closer to the Lord.

DAD .....

I am not sure when Dad's last day on earth was in his own mind. Doctors may say one thing and family members who were there may say another. It doesn't matter when the last day was for him, but I would like to tell you what I think happened on that day.

He awakened early in the morning as always, dressed, made his coffee, and sat down at the kitchen table to spend time with his Lord, Savior, and best friend, Jesus, who met him every morning as he had for so many years. His old Bible was worn and bent and well used, but Jesus met him in there every morning. They visited, talked as old friends do, and then Mom would get up and join them with coffee and the fellowship with her Lord and her two best friends. After their morning visit Mom would cook their breakfast and then the day would get down to its normal pattern. Dad never left the house in the morning without his friend Jesus. Their relationship was so close and strong that I believe Jesus took extra care of all of Dad's family the same way. With everything going on there on the farm, with all we had to do, no matter who was outside working, whether up in the silo, in the barns, working in the field, working with the big equipment, no matter what, Jesus never allowed any of Dad's kids to be alone and in danger. After their breakfast was finished

Dad would kiss Mom good-bye as "he and Jesus" headed out the door to take care of his "never-ending" list of chores. Where he and Jesus went that day I have no idea, what they did I do not know for that day belonged to Dad and Jesus. Did they traverse the caves and canyons of Dad's memory? Did they walk past the old Cary School and look in the windows of his childhood? Did they walk past Emil Bauer's farm and watch the kids from years ago working and playing and spend some time visiting with Andy, his best friend? Dad and his best friend had married sisters and had been best of friends for well over 70 years. Did they visit places from World War II that maybe stood out in Dad's mind for one reason or another? Did he and his brother Ed go to town for a visit, or maybe sit on the creek bank and tell stories of the old days, did Dad and Mom maybe go to one of the ballrooms in Chicago where they spent an evening once in a while, taking the train to and from, enjoying being young and in love, and planning their future and their family, and dream of what could be. Did he and Jesus go down to Otto Knoll's and shock oats, go past Kenneth Hammerton's and pitch bundles into the threshing machine or top-off the straw stack as he had so many years ago, or did they walk down to Swing Elevator and sit in the office and visit with old friends as they passed through? Names from the past, faces in the mist, voices in the dark, people who had influenced Dad and many he had influenced himself; names like Dwight Leigh, Glenn Strom, Harry Hoffman, Walt Johnson, Lawrence Leigh, Ray Eisenmann, Marv Swing, Art Smiley, Harry Magee, Ralph Knapp, Elmer Burgett, Herman Bauer, just some of the names from the past, names of those with whom he had grown-up, good friends, faces, jokes, fellowship, that which makes a lifetime of good living worth it all. Who knows, maybe they walked over towards the town of Rankin and walked past the Fred Schupbach farm, looking to see whether Fred's daughter Anna Marie was outside and they could visit a few minutes. She was his love for many years and the mother of his children...

They walked and talked, as good friends do, about the same things good friends do, until it got late into the day and the breeze stopped, the air calmed, and the shadows lengthened. They stopped and Dad turned to his friend and said, "it's getting late, we need to turn around and head back to Fountain Creek, Mom will have supper ready pretty soon and we don't want to be late for that, whatever it is it will be good and we don't want to miss it, we'll hear her calling pretty soon." Jesus looked at Dad and put his hand on his shoulder and said, "my friend, my dear friend, it's been a long trip, sometimes the road was smooth, sometimes it was rocky, sometimes flat and sometimes uphill, sometimes a wide open path and sometimes a winding path with steep ditches, sometimes hot, sometimes cold, but no matter what, it has been a long trip and we have managed it well and it has been my thrill and pleasure to have accompanied you on your trip. It is indeed a long way back home to Fountain Creek, to your home. Why don't you just come home with me tonight, we are much closer to my home than we are to yours? In my Father's house are many mansions, if it were not so I would have told you." Dad looked at his friend and asked, "what about Mom, I need to talk to her, I need to tell her what's going on, she'll be looking for us." Jesus looked at his friend and said "she is fine my friend, my Father has sent a Comforter to her, she is aware of what is going on and she knows she will see you again soon, and I will be with her again in the morning for our visit and I will continue to see her every day until it is her time to come home to you, Me, and my Father." At this time Dad and his friend Jesus turned and looked back at the farm at Fountain Creek and Dad saw Mom standing outside the porch looking at him, and as he watched, a mist formed around the farm, covering all but his beautiful wife of so many years. As he watched, she was joined by his son Vic, his first-born, his heir, his son, every father's pride, who would work so hard and become so much because of the lessons he learned at his father's side as a child on the farm. As Vic took his place behind and beside his mother it brought a satisfied smile to his worn, worried and tired face. As he watched, they were joined by Rog, his second son, the wanderer who wanted so much to be half the man his father was. They stood behind their mother, wanting so much to be her strength and to protect her from all of life's troubles and problems, as he himself had tried to do for so many years, smiling and looking at him in the distance. Again the mist parted and Velma walked through and stood beside her mother; his first daughter, a father's dream; a daughter, a little girl to raise and protect and love, a daughter who would be as outspoken and as opinionated as he was and it brought another smile to his face. He looked again and the mist parted again and his daughter Alice walked through and stood beside her mother. His daughter Alice, his little girl who was born on the birthday of his best friend Jesus, Alice, his Christmas baby who meant so much to him. She stood on the other side of Mom and Dad looked and was so happy that Mom was in the middle of his two daughters, so much like him and so much like their mother and he was happy and content that Mom would be well taken care of. The mist parted again and through the swirl walked Jeff, his son who was such a friend, such a companion, always there to help, always there to offer to go wherever they needed, ready to drive to wherever Dad and Mom needed to go or wanted to go to see some of the kids or grandkids and always such a fan of the family. He took his place with the rest of the kids surrounding their mother and wanting to protect her. The mist rolled again, swirling around the family and the farm in the background and Marv walked out; the son who would be so much more than just a son to his father, the son who would be a partner, the son on whom he would lean and ask so much advice. The one who was so strong, a farmer, the strengths that he himself enjoyed as a young man, the one who had enough strength to give the extra to Dad during the planting and harvesting seasons, the times a farmer lives for, the one who also had the love of the land, the love of the crops, the love of knowing the only thing they could add to their farm was the tremendous faith that God will bring the needed rain and the crops would grow. As he looked fondly back the mists once again swirled and parted and out walked Harry, his youngest, the one who brought so much delight to him when he would come and spend a day. He remembered the visits as they drove the farmstead, the laughing, and the reminiscing they did as they talked and laughed and were so close. As he walked into the midst of the family group, Harry leaned down and kissed his mother and then took his place at the family's side, there to do all they could for their mother as their father traveled on to a better place, Jesus' house. As he looked, tears formed in Dad's eyes as he realized that he and Mom had done the best they could and now, when needed, as they had hoped for as they raised their family, all the kids were there to surround their mother with love and do all possible to help her in the times of sadness and loneliness and although they would never replace the man she had lost, they would do their best to make sure her days were happy, safe, and she was loved. Dad stood and looked back, it was hard to see through the fog, was it his eyes or was it the mist surrounding his memory, or was it knowing that he would see them all again, in due time, and until then, he would be at home with his friend, his Lord, his Savior, his God, in Heaven, which he had often dreamed of as he pondered Paradise. The mist began to close over the family and he looked once more, his eyes cleared, he saw Mom and waved, a long, loving wave, and Mom waved back and he heard her still, soft, quiet voice say, "I love you, thanks for the years and know that I will think of you constantly until we meet again. Good-bye my love, my husband, my friend." Dad whispered back with his voice cracking and failing and said, "I love you, thanks for loving me and I will wait for you to join me again." The wind stirred, the mist rolled and covered the family from Dad's eyes and he turned to his good friend Jesus and smiled through the tears and they turned and walked, arm in arm, through the Eastern Gate of Heaven, to Glory, to Paradise, where there is no pain and where there are no more tears. There to meet those who have gone before and to wait for those still to come.

Although it has nothing to do with the circumstances, there is a verse in I Samuel that fits so well. It is where Jonathon and David are speaking of Jonathon's father, King Saul, and his growing hate of David. Although not of related matters, I Samuel 20:18 expresses all that needs to be said of Dad. "Then Jonathon said to David, Tomorrow is the new moon: and thou shalt be missed, because thy seat will be empty." We love you Dad, and you will be missed, tremendously, "because thy seat will be empty," and there is none to fill it. Good-bye Dad, we love you and we will see you again.

Precious memories, how they linger, how they ever thrill my soul.... In the stillness of the midnight, precious sacred scenes unfold .....

Thanks for everything Dad; we love you, Vic, Rog, Velma, Alice, Jeff, Marv and Harry

Mom ...

Mom wasn't quite sure what had awakened her so early that morning. Was it the dream again or was it the soft light in her room that seemed to be coming from nowhere, yet was everywhere. She thought about the dream again. Dad had come to her in her dreams during her sleep quite often during the 4+ years since he had died, and she always awakened with a happy feeling, yet more of an alone feeling than before. They had been married almost 60 years and had become one and the same in every sense of the word. She missed him, terribly, and wanted to go home to Heaven, this world just wasn't the same without Dad. This dream was different though as she thought about it. Usually Dad had come and sat on the edge of the bed and they visited. He always looked the way she remembered him, with his worn, weathered, lined and wrinkled face, his tired smile, his gray hair, his worn and weathered arms. Like all dreams, we remember what we knew. This morning's dream was different though. He was dressed in a white robe, a shining white robe, and he looked the way she remembered him when they were young. When he came home on leave from the Army during World War II and had proposed to her. He was young, his hair was black again, his arms were smooth and strong, no lines in his face, his eyes sparkling, his smile was wide and he looked extremely happy and

7

content. He had not stayed long though. He hovered above the bed and called her name softly until she awakened, then they smiled at each other and Dad said he couldn't stay, but they would be together again, very soon.

It was after he left that she noticed the light in the room beginning to shine. She noticed that the room was even brighter now, and the light seemed to be coming from right in the middle of the room, in the mid-air. She reached for it, but couldn't reach the light, but she noticed her arm as she reached: it was young and full and strong and smooth again, as it had been before time began playing tricks on her body as it does with all of us. She raised her other arm, turned her hands and looked at what she used to look like, and then she felt her face and it was young and smooth again, and she felt her head of hair and it was long as it had been before and she could hold it out and saw that it was a shade of brown and auburn which she hadn't seen for years. She looked back at the light coming from the center of the room, saw the outline of a man forming, and she knew, right then, as she watched, she knew ... Jesus was coming for her. That explained the short visit from Dad, somehow God had given him permission to tell Mom it was her time, that explained the youthful appearance of her skin and body again, she was going home to Heaven, and the Light was Jesus, and that explained everything. As she watched, smiling broadly, waiting expectantly, Jesus smiled at her and she realized that her every thought all of her life as to what Jesus would be couldn't begin to explain what it was really like to see him face to face. Mom smiled and said, "Hello Lord, I've been waiting for you and I'm glad you're here." Jesus smiled and said that it wasn't quite her time yet, she wouldn't leave for Heaven with him till later that evening and none of the kids would be there to see her leave, but they would all know where she had gone, but that because of her faithfulness and the love the Father has for her, Jesus had come to spend her last day on earth with her, to grant her each and every wish she might have. Whatever she wanted to do, wherever she wanted to go, she had but to ask and it would be granted, and she and Jesus would spend the day, the last day of her life here on earth, together.

As she thought about it she realized how good her life had been, from her childhood on the farm with the family she loved, through school, through college, her teaching jobs in Jacksonville and Peoria, her marriage to Dad, her family, all seven of the children whom she loved dearly, everything, she had been blessed richly and had no idea where she could possibly want to go now that it was over other than to Heaven. She realized that she would like to see her family again and asked Jesus if it were possible to go back to the farm where she had been born and raised with her brothers and sisters, and spend part of a day with them. She no more than got the question out of her mouth than she and Jesus were standing on the edge of the lawn of the front yard on the farm outside of Rankin. Jesus assured her that she could not be seen or heard so she was free to wander and visit the canyons of her memory and enjoy the time and that He would be right there beside her.

She heard children laughing and began to walk towards the house and saw the four little girls come around the corner of the house, running and chasing and she stopped and looked at them and realized that the little girls were her sisters Lucille, Frieda and the youngest, little Rosella, and that the fourth was her; Mom herself, as a young girl. She smiled when she saw the little blue play dress that Frieda was wearing. She remembered her mom making that for her older sister Esther a few years back and couldn't wait until Esther outgrew it so she could wear it. She loved that dress and now here was Frieda wearing it. Oh the memories! She watched them play, listening to them laugh and talk and giggle and again she remembered the wonderful childhood with the wonderful family God had given her.

9

She heard voices back behind the house and slowly walked toward the tool shed, looking at the garden which she remembered so well, the flowers that her mother had loved, the trees she had climbed, the source of many a skinned knee and shin. As she approached the shed she saw her brothers, Walt and George, working on one of the farm implements and heard voices from inside the shed. As she walked from the sunlight into the darkness inside the shed she saw her dad and her brother Eddie and heard him teasing his dad asking him to yodel for him again. The flood of memories staggered her and she had to stop and get her balance and breath. Her dad, she hadn't seen him for over fifty years, since he had passed away and she didn't remember him looking so young and strong and she laughed at Eddie wanting him to yodel. She would have loved to hear that herself again. She wondered, but didn't dare ask Jesus something so silly, as to whether or not she could hear her dad yodel in Heaven, but Jesus, being God, and knowing everything smiled and said, without her asking, "Yes, he does yodel sometimes in Heaven for your mom, your brothers, and some of your sisters who are there now." He took off his hat to wipe his brow and Mom stepped closer and kissed him lightly on the cheek. He smiled and looked at his youngest son, Eddie and said "an angel just kissed me" and he smiled and began to yodel for a few seconds, bringing a smile to Eddie's face and appreciative chuckles from Walt and George working on the equipment.

A small gust of wind brought a smell to the shed from the house and Mom walked slowly away from the shed onto the front porch and into the kitchen, where her sisters Clara and Esther were rolling, kneading, cutting and baking cinnamon rolls. The smell Mom knew so well and remembered so well from her childhood. Today had to be Saturday, tomorrow would be Sunday and her dad always enjoyed cinnamon rolls on Sunday before they got ready for church. She looked at the stove and there stood her mom, her mother, the woman she loved so much who had taught her so well how to be a good wife and mother. She wondered if her mother knew what an influence she had been and again, Jesus answered without being asked, "Yes, she has realized what a blessing she was to her children, the Father has told her and showed her." Her mom was stirring a pot of soup and singing softly under her breath, an old gospel song, in German. Mom recognized the song and wished she could join her in singing. She stood in the kitchen enjoying the sights and smells for a few more minutes, whispered to her mom, "I love you" and started to leave. Her sisters looked at their mom and asked what was wrong as they had never seen that expression before. Her mom said she wasn't sure but she just had the nicest, softest and warmest feeling of overwhelming love cross her mind and it just felt so good, like the touch of an angel. Mom and Jesus walked out into the front yard, near the playing girls and Jesus asked where she wanted to go next.

She asked if it would be possible to visit a few places from school days and immediately she was walking towards a school bus parked outside the high school she had attended. As she stepped up on the steps to enter the bus she heard "Anne, Anne, over here, I saved you a place." She knew right away it was Dad, years before they had married. Although they had never dated during school, they were always close and he had always saved her a seat if they were going somewhere on the same bus. She smiled and thanked Jesus and he just smiled back. Just like that they were in Jacksonville, where she was teaching and it was a Friday evening and she was very happy. Dad was home on leave from WWII and coming to see her this weekend. She was happy and excited as they had become very close the past few years with him off to war and she teaching school away from home. The letters had been a calming sanity for both of them during a very troubling time. As she and Jesus watched time pass, she saw Dad driving towards her house and she ran out to meet him, she hadn't seen him for a long time and he was going to take her to see her folks back home. As he got out of the car they hugged for a long time, Dad kissed her and asked her to marry him. Without a second hesitation she said "yes" and they left to tell her folks.

Jesus asked where she wanted to go next and Mom asked if it would be possible to visit each of her children since they wouldn't be there when she left and Jesus said that would be no problem and once again they were off. She spent the rest of the afternoon visiting each of her children, spending time with each of them and enjoying every minute of the time, knowing that she had done her best with them, and happy and content with what they were doing and how they had turned out as grown adults.

When the afternoon shadows were lengthening Jesus told her it was time to return to her room to prepare to leave and He asked how the time was with the children. She smiled and thanked him so much, so sincerely, and she told Him about the visits. She said she watched each of her daughters going about their daily tasks, so proud of them and the way they had turned out, so happy with them. She said she watched her older son in his office, talking and making decisions and he reminded her so much of Dad, he had learned well. She had spent time with her youngest son at his position in the control room of the processing plant, so knowing and so confident in his position, so sure of himself from the upbringing he had received from his dad. She commented that although she had never ridden in a truck while she was younger and able, she had ridden with all three of her other boys in their trucks now, on this, her last day and she had enjoyed every ride and every mile. She understood their attraction to the job and she wished she had tried it earlier.

As they returned to her room in the hospital, they hovered above the bed, watching the scene unfold below. A doctor was holding her arm, feeling for a pulse that ceased to exist and he said, "It's over, she's gone, she now belongs to the ages." Mom looked at Jesus and smiled a happy smile, even with the "good-bye" tears in her eyes and said "Thank-you Jesus, it was a beautiful, blessed life." Jesus smiled back, took Mom's arm, they turned towards Heaven and He said, "This has been nothing, my Father awaits you now in Eternal Glory and you can't even begin to imagine what is awaiting you." Mom smiled, trying to imagine what awaited her, and she smiled as she thought of passing through the pearly gates of Heaven and hearing that old familiar voice saying softly, "Anne, Anne, over here, I've saved you a place."

… and shout while passing through the air, farewell, farewell, sweet hour of prayer …

Thank-you Mom, we love you, Vic, Rog, Velma, Alice, Jeff, Marv and Harry …..

CREATION

The gospel of John, chapter 1, verse 1 says, "In the beginning was the Word, and the Word was with God, and the Word was God." Verse 3 says, "All things were made by him; and without him was not anything made that was made." Jesus is the Word of God, and Jesus was the One who created all things. There it is, in black and white. Jesus created all that was created. I like the Bible, the written word of God. There are so many verses, chapters, books and stories that all add up to Jesus, and I enjoy reading each of them, time and again. I don't care how many times I read each of them; they are always new and exciting and show me something I did not see the last time I read them. I love John 3:16, Hebrews 10:12, Revelations 22:20, and Luke 23:43 just to name a few. There are also two other parts of verses that mean so much to me. In Genesis chapter one both are found. "And God said …" and also "… and God saw that it was good." Two of my favorite examples of the might and power of God, right there in those short, few words. The entire universe and all that is in it were created by the spoken word of God. "And God said …" and creation happened. God spoke and perfection happened. Out of nothing He made everything, perfectly, the first time. There were no corrections, no redo, no problems; all was perfect the first time, every time. "… and God saw that it was good." What a testimony to, and a perfect example of, the perfection of God. After each of the first five days of creation this verse appears, and after the sixth day, the final day of creation, it says, "and God looked and saw that it was very good." There is none above God, none is His equal. There is none to judge God, so God judges God, and He judges God perfect. God cannot tell a lie, cannot make a mistake, cannot change His mind, and is always true to His word and His promises. God; God the Father, God the Son, and God the Holy Spirit, is perfect and cannot be anything but perfect. God has been forever and will be forever. His kingdom has been here forever and will never end, and we will join Him in His kingdom to live for eternity. God, who created us out of the dust of the earth and formed us by hand, created us perfect. We sinned and yet God does not judge us by His perfection standards. We are judged and justified by His son Jesus, and His righteousness.

A short while back as I was driving down the highway and just finishing my morning prayers, my mind began wandering through the stories and the books in my mind and I began thinking of the Creation. We all know the order of creation, we can find that in Genesis, not a problem, but I began thinking of the wonder of creation. We don't know for sure when the angels were created. Everything else is spelled out and easy to understand, but the specific creation of the angels is not stated. I have read of those who believe the first day when God created light, although the sun wasn't created for a few days yet, that the "light" was the angels. I don't know. Evidently God didn't think that was important enough to expound upon. It doesn't matter, at least not to me. The angels were a special creation, to serve and glorify God and to be His messengers. They are His and His alone. I'm happy just knowing they are here and they are part of God's creation, and they are the only witnesses to the creation of the universe, and all that is in it, and all that will be until God is finished with it.

Here is where I enjoy my "wandering" mind. I realize that what I write here is not in the specific, correct order of creation, but is my enjoyment of the creation. Can you picture the joy and excitement of the angels as they saw things appear where there had been nothing? Can you picture them watching on day 3 when God separated the waters, making lakes, oceans, rivers and streams? Having separated the waters, land now appeared. Water, land, what are these things we see here before us? What is this, what great things hath God wrought? Living things were made to grow on the land. Not all sprouted from seeds; that would have taken too long. There were full grown trees, patches of wild flowers, grass on the flatland prairies, cactus, roses, lily pads on the calm waters, beautiful bushes, weathered and beaten trees on the high mountains; every kind of living plant. We know that angels have senses. They can see, they rejoice when a soul is saved, and I can picture them smelling the flowers, feeling the bushes, and feeling the thorns on a cactus. It wouldn't hurt them, they have no physical bodies, but they enjoyed the creation. I can picture the mighty archangel Michael as he cupped the first rose he saw in his mighty warrior's hand, or ran the tall grass between his fingers, or marveled at the first apple he ever saw on a tree. I wonder if he tasted a strawberry or pulled up and tasted a carrot. I can hear them shouting at one another, "come see this, come smell this flower, come feel this cool water, look at these blossoms," and so much more. I can see them approaching the Throne of God in their excitement, shining, and I can see God smiling at their rejoicing and praising; thinking to Himself that they had seen nothing yet.

Picture them on day 4, when all of a sudden the sun appeared. Where there had been nothing before, now there was a huge, burning ball of fire. In the vacuum of space, with no oxygen, where a fire is impossible, now hung the sun, burning brightly. "Look, over there, what is that ball of light that has no power source?" "It is the moon; the light comes from the sun shining on it, but look at all those stars." The sun, the moon, and the stars, placed where God wanted each of them to be. The earth, all the planets, everything put in such perfection that man was able to distinguish time. The length of a day, the length of time of a year, all time in such a way that even man can understand. There is no clock or calendar in Heaven; God doesn't need that for His time is perfect, always. Each star placed perfectly, and God knows the name of each star, each one. And the angels laughed and shouted, praising God, and examining the creation of the One who created them, and again I can see the Heavenly Father smiling at their joy. You hear all of the scientists and the non-believers talking about the "big bang" theory. I would say there was plenty of "bang" on each day of creation. I don't think a ball of fire such as the sun, or a star, or the moon entered the universe any too quietly and I don't think God was sneaking anything in, I believe there was more than one "big bang" as creation happened.

How about the excitement and joy and hollering and celebrating and praising God on day 5, when all of a sudden there were fishes in the waters, and birds in the air? I can see angels hovering in the air and all of a sudden there were birds flying by. "Hey, look at that, they can fly, like us." I don't believe all the birds were created standing on the ground, nor were all the fishes created lying on the bottom of the body of water they were in. I believe birds were created flying, perching on tree branches, singing, doing what birds do, and I believe there were some created sitting on a nest of eggs that were created at the same time. How the angels must have rejoiced and celebrated when they heard all the different songs and sounds from the birds, what music to their ears. I can see their amazement as they watch a flock of chickens scratching the dirt, and wondered at the first chicken eggs they saw, or watched a peacock spread it's beautiful tail. I believe the fishes were created swimming in the water. I can see the angels looking at a group of goldfish swimming by in a small pool of water, watching a frog sitting on a lily pad and then jumping into the water, and watching a whale swim by. Again, I can see God smiling as He listened to the angels celebrating what was happening. Again, the angels were the only witnesses to creation and I believe they enjoyed it tremendously.

Then came day 6, the final day of creation, when all the other animals were created. Can you picture their amazement and surprise as they saw monkeys swinging in the trees, or herds of buffalo grazing in the grass on the prairies, or watched a new-born calf, or a brand new litter of pigs, or a new colt following it's mother around, or a grizzly bear with her cubs looking for food for them, or hear the wonder in their voices as they try to figure the neck of a giraffe? They had to stand in "open-mouthed" amazement for a few moments before they began to smile, laugh and celebrate this new "magical, mystical miracle." Again I smile at the thought of the archangel Michael as he watched his first kangaroo hop by. Do you think he reached for his sword wondering just exactly what this was? Can you picture the mighty Archangel holding his first kitten, or do you think the warrior in him would have appreciated a wolf cub even a little more, or maybe a pride of lions with their young? I picture angels sitting in the grass holding little kittens, puppies, skunks and porcupines and laughing with glee, and again I picture God smiling at their celebration and the praise of His creation. And then, also on day 6, God said, "Let us make man in our image." I don't know if man was created standing, sitting or lying, but I know he was made out of the dust of the earth, by hand, the hands of God, and that man was everything that God wanted him to be. When God was finished He breathed life into man and man lived, walked, talked and could reason. God later put man into a deep sleep, took one of his ribs and created woman the same way. When man and woman were both living and breathing, they could communicate. I have no idea what language they spoke, but they were created with the ability to speak, hear and understand each other. This was a perfect creation by the perfect Creator, and witnessed by the angels: Absolute perfection in each and every way. We have fallen a long way, but we were created perfectly.

This is such a short story, but I can think, and could write a book on the miracles of the creation of the universe and all that is in it by our God, our Heavenly Father. No, I don't believe in evolution of the species as the beginning of life, the earth and the universe, my faith isn't that strong. I have heard that people think creation is so hard to believe. Not for me, I can believe in creation a whole lot easier than I can believe we all came from one freak, accidental, single-cell, which apparently came from nowhere and managed to make all of this. No, little too hard for me to believe, I'll go with the creation story from my God, my Heavenly Father.

There are so many things that I would like to see when I get to Heaven, and I hope that God will let me watch the Creation story. All things are possible with God, so maybe He'll let me see it. I want to watch it, shout with glee and praise God for His miracles as I believe the angels did as they watched perfection happen. Out of nothing God made everything. God spoke and perfection happened. The angels witnessed this; we can read of it in the first chapters of Genesis, in the written Word of God and picture it as beautifully as the angels saw it. I thank you so much God for your faithfulness and your perfection and your forgiveness and for your love. I thank-you for Jesus who bore the righteous wrath of God in my place, and traded His perfect, pure life for my sin-filled life, and who assured me of my future in Heaven; forever with my Creator, my owner, my

Redeemer, the God of my salvation, my Lord, my God, my friend, my everything.

He's got the whole world, in His hands He's got the whole wide world, in His hands He's got the whole world, in His hands He's got the whole world in His hands …

EXCUSE ME MISTER ...

"Excuse me mister, but are you God?" I was sitting at a table in the food court at the mall having a cup of coffee and reading my paper, wasting time before I picked up the few things I needed at one of the stores when I heard the small voice ask the question. I looked up and saw a small boy holding a smaller girl's hand at the table next to me, where an older gentleman was sitting, also reading his paper. "Excuse me mister," he asked again, "but are you God?" The old man finished folding his paper, laid it on the table and then looked at the young boy and girl. "No young fellow, I am not God, but He is a good friend of mine and we visit several times a day. Is there anything I can do for you and what lead you to ask me if I was God?" "My name is Billy, I am six years old and this is my little sister Carol, she's only four." We can't find our daddy and Daddy and Mommy always told us that whenever we have a problem God will help us. We needed help and thought you might be God, Daddy always said He was an old man with a white beard and was real nice, we thought that was how you looked." The old man chuckled and sat the youngsters down on two of the chairs at his table and asked what had happened leading to this problem.

21

"Well," Billy started, "Daddy brought us to the mall with him right after we had our lunch and sat us at a table. He gave us a hot chocolate to drink and said he would be right back as soon as he could." I saw the old man look at his watch and then saw his face fall as he thought the same thing I was thinking. The kids had already been here a few hours, was this another case of child abandonment? I could see he didn't have the heart to even mention that as a possibility so he asked the usual questions: what does Daddy look like, what kind of clothes is he wearing, what way did he go when he left you here, do you know what he wanted to buy, what store he would be going to; all questions to kill time as he searched his mind for answers. He went to the counter and bought a milk and a cookie for each of them, brought them back to the table and told the kids that as soon as they were finished eating them they would all go and search for their Daddy. He had said that he and God were friends and visited several times a day. I could see in his face that this was one of the times and it was in earnest. He kept up the conversation to keep the kids' minds off of the situation and soon they finished the milk and cookies and were ready to go look for their Daddy.

The mall was set up like a large "X" with the food court in the center so as they went down one of the major aisles looking in all the stores, coming back towards the middle looking on the other side of the aisle I could follow their progress all the way. The old man was carrying little Carol on his shoulders and holding little Billy's hand and I could see by his face as they approached the food court again for the third time, only one more major aisle to go, that he wasn't expecting any better luck this time either. It was pretty well obvious what had happened although I didn't want to think it and he sure didn't want to mention it to the children. Soon enough they reached the far end of the last aisle and turned to come back on the other side, checking the stores there. I could hear them singing "Jesus Loves Me," a song the kids had obviously learned in Sunday School and one probably known by the old man for his entire life as they walked the last leg back to the food court. The old man had done well, he had wasted an entire hour on the search, time to give anyone a chance to come back if they were going to. They came backs to the same table, next to mine, and sat back down. The old man tried to keep it light as he told the kids that he need more help to find their daddy, so they would sing one more chorus of "Jesus Loves Me" and then he would go find a policeman or the mall security to help them find Daddy. I looked at my watch and realized that it had been three or four hours minimum since their dad had left them at the mall. They started to sing again and I found myself singing along with them, with tears running down my face as I felt the pain, which would soon enough encompass all of them. They were just finishing the song when I heard shouting way off in the distance, "Billy, Carol, Billy, Carol, please kids, still be here." A few seconds later a man came running into the food court and you knew instantly from the look on his face and smiles on the kids' faces that dad had come back for them, as he had said and as they had not doubted. After hugging them for several seconds he finally looked at the old man and with tears in his eyes asked, "excuse me mister, but are you God?"

The young man pulled up a chair at the table and told the old man that he owed him an explanation if he had the time to listen. The old man told him that all he had was time so please go on. The young man was an HVAC technician but had lost his job about three months ago when the business closed down and he had been unable to find employment anywhere else. His wife, the children's mother had been sick for some time and had passed away only a month ago and he just couldn't take any more. He was defeated, tired and ready to give up. He had no other family to take care of the kids so he had put a slip of paper in the pocket of their jackets with their names and address on them, and taken them to the mall. He figured that two kids that small would soon enough draw attention and the security would call the police who would call the child welfare people and eventually the kids would be taken into an office somewhere safe to be questioned. Once there their names and address would be found, a car would be dispatched to the address and they would find his body, along with a long letter he had written explaining why he had done this. It wasn't what he wanted but he knew the kids would be safe and he figured in better hands than his poor unemployed condition would provide. He had just finished the letter, set it on the table, drank the last couple of swallows out of a bottle of whiskey he had saved for this occasion, filled his hand with the sleeping pills he planned to take, laid down on the couch when all of a sudden, as clear as if it were on a television right in front of him he saw the inside of the mall and he saw God walking the halls, his daughter Carol on His shoulder and his son Billy holding His hand, and all of them singing "Jesus Loves Me." He said he watched this for a couple of minutes until the magnitude of what he was doing sunk into his mind and he sat bolt upright hollering "NO!" at the top of his lungs. He jumped into his car and raced back to the mall, hoping his children were still there. All the while he told the story he was crying and hugging the kids.

When everything had finally calmed down, the young man had regained his composure, the kids relaxed and played kid games at the table, the old man took out a pen and paper and wrote the name and address of a business on it. He explained to the young man that this was his old company, controlled now by his son, and they needed help. He was an HVAC contractor who had just recently won a couple of large contracts and was in need of some good experienced help. At the bottom of the note he added, "Son, hire this man immediately, I can attest to his ability, honesty and integrity.

See you soon, love Dad." He told the young man to give this to the boss, his son, and to have a good life and enjoy the job. Everyone got up, going his or her own way and soon after I also followed, going to my car and back to my own home.

Postscript: About a week and a half later as I was reading the Sunday paper I came across the obituary section. I always look through It just to see if I know anyone. There, the second obit was the picture of the old man in the mall, along with the typical things about his life as you read in all of them. He had finished the work God had for him and now had taken him home. Two different people, a young boy and the young boy's father had asked him within about three hours of each other if he was God. "No, we are good friends though." I chuckled as I read his name and the irony of his initials: Galen Oral Doggins.

"They left one by one ... as their work here was done ... gone home, gone home ...

FOUNTAIN CREEK

I miss the small local hamlets, villages or even towns should you want to call them that. Years ago railroad sidings would spring up from the prairie, like the corn, wheat and oats the "westward" moving settlers were planting all over the heartland of America, in the Midwest, the "grain" belt. Farmers shipped their crops from these locations. The small "sidings" usually consisted of a grain elevator, probably a blacksmith shop, a church, a few houses, maybe a general store, and sometimes until the late 1930's or 1940's, even a small, one-room grade school for the local children to attend. I am not talking about a small town by our standards today, but rather a town of usually less than 100 people, along the railroad lines, where the inhabitants were more family than just neighbors and friends. This is where I come from and I miss my home; where I was born.

I was born only a half a mile from one of these small "sidings" and recently have realized how much a part of my life it is. Fountain Creek, Illinois is a small grain elevator on the siding of the railroad one half of a mile west of the farmstead where we seven kids were born and raised (the same farm house where my father was born and raised) and lived our lives in blissful ignorance of the big, cold world that awaited us. There is only one house in Fountain Creek now,

Sam Ristow and his family are the sole inhabitants of the siding, Sam is the "all in one" Mayor, Police force, city council and most of all, citizen. At one time in my youth there were four houses in Fountain Creek. A total of four families lived in the small village. It was home to them and also the "center of the universe" to many more of us. My father passed away on 16 January 2006, and left his farmstead in his own personal Fountain Creek, and his funeral took place on Friday, 20 January 2006. During the funeral service the minister made mention of the fact that "you can take the boy out of Fountain Creek but you can never take Fountain Creek out of the boy." My father spent all but four years of his life in the house one half of a mile east of Fountain Creek. He was in the United States Army from 1942 through 1945, as most of his generation, fighting and winning World War II. He was part of Tom Brokaw's "The Greatest Generation" and it was his honor to have served in the military during the war. The thoughts and dreams of his fiancé, and the thoughts of his Fountain Creek and the farm; the land he was born on, kept him company and helped keep his sanity during the insanity of war, and brought him home after the war. This story is not about my father, but rather Fountain Creek. Not just the one in my life, but all of the Fountain Creeks, in everyone's lives; in all of the states, regions, counties and localities that dot the landscape of this America.

The store in Fountain Creek had closed before I was born, but while still open it was the kind of place that when my father was a child his mother sent his younger brother, my Uncle Ed, to the store to "get the bill" so she could pay the storekeeper what she owed. Not entirely understanding the term "bill," young Eddie got on his bike, rode the half-mile, walked into the store and told the storekeeper, "Mom needs a dollar bill." Although the storekeeper didn't know what was going on, he figured that Tillie Gudeman must need a dollar for something so he gave young Eddie a dollar bill to take home to his mother. When Uncle Ed got to the house and gave the dollar to his mother and she figured out what had transpired he was promptly sent back down on his bicycle and returned the dollar and brought home the "bill" Grandma was looking for. We need to return to that kind of trust and friendship. I miss that style of neighbor.

In my own "Fountain Creek" there are so many similar stories. You would go on a vacation or a long weekend visit somewhere and when you returned home you would find a bottle of ketchup or maybe a sack of sugar or some other grocery product on your table. Without knowing the story you would put it in the pantry where it belonged and before too long, maybe a few days, one of the neighbors would ask if you found it. Your comment would be "yes, we wondered where it came from?" She would laugh and say that she was baking something, making a special supper or whatever, and needed one or two more of the ingredients. It was a few miles to the store and "I knew you had some in your pantry so I came in and got it, when I went to the store a couple of days later I got a new one and put it on your table so you would know that you were out in the pantry." As a young man I went "over the road" as a truck driver in 1974. At that time I installed a lock on the front door of my house for my family's safety. Until that time there had never been a lock on the door, and it was only used then on the nights that I was gone, and when I returned the door remained unlocked until I left again. I miss that style of life and security.

When I was a young man at home on the farm I saved my money one year to buy my dad a special Christmas present. I had saved what I considered to be a reasonable amount of money and went to the local tractor dealer to purchase the Christmas present. I so proudly told the man behind the parts counter, who happened to be the owner, how much I had saved and what I wished to get and for what reason. He looked up the parts and told me the cost and amazingly enough I had saved just a few more dollars than needed. I made the purchase and received my change and left, happy. It was several years later that I was told by another employee of the dealership the truth of my purchase. I had not saved enough for the gift but in his "Fountain Creek" style of life, the owner had sold the gift to me for what I had saved. A short time after Christmas my dad was in the dealership for parts and was asked if he had enjoyed the gift he was given. Dad responded how much he had and then was told the rest of the story. My dad paid for the rest of his own gift and never mentioned it to me. I miss that style of life.

We didn't have fences as property lines in our Fountain Creek. Yards were there for all to enjoy and use if needed. I always enjoyed the agreement my next-door neighbor and I had. The property line was decided by who mowed their yard first. If I got out there before he did I would mow a strip down the side of my house and he would have to mow over to it when he mowed. If he mowed first, he would make one strip down the side of his house and the rest of the yard was mine to mow. Was an easy agreement and the rules were quite simple and it worked well for us for years. I wonder how they do it now. I have driven by the houses several times when I go home for a visit but have not seen them mowing. Hope it is still as easy as it was then.

Fountain Creek is the place where neighbors are there for you. I remember one dairy farmer who was severely hurt one fall in an accident. His farm work was finished by all of the neighbors and his dairy herd was tended and cared for and milked on schedule until he was able to return to his work himself and there was no bill, nothing owed, and nothing expected. They were neighbors. Another farmer was injured in a tractor accident and received a broken leg. He was laid up, unable to man his equipment and do the harvest of the crops on which he depended for his living. Neighbors left their fields to take care of his crops. There were combines and tractors and wagons and the crops were harvested and the fields were plowed and then the neighbors returned to their own fields and crops. How many bills today do moist eyes and heartfelt thanks pay? How many bills of that magnitude would be paid by a simple dinner served to all the farmers who came to help? There is a saying I heard from my father quite often that I have always loved and used myself now and then: "thanks a lot until you're better paid." I miss the love, thoughtfulness, kindness and friendship that is and was a part of that life.

Although there really is a place called Fountain Creek, I have come to realize that more than a physical location it is a "way of life" or even a "peace of mind" if you please. There are many more folks out there than just I who came from small locations like this. They are fading away as more and more people are leaving rural America for the cities and towns where the thoughts of a better life may leave them with more money in their pockets at the end of a week or month, but at what cost? Farming has turned into a large business where one must now farm hundreds if not thousands of acres to make a substantial living, leaving many on the small family farms to abandon their own "Fountain Creek" in favor of a life in the city. I dare say there is a still small flickering flame in many people to return to the better days, slower ways, friendly neighbors, trust and friendship, and a much more relaxed and happy lifestyle.

There is the story from long ago which I did not understand when I was a child, but after being gone for the military, moving several times for work, etc. the story has a very serious meaning to me. It is one of those stories that you wish were true when you think of it. The story goes that a young salesman stopped one day at Swing Elevator, the grain elevator in Fountain Creek. There was a red payphone hanging on the wall with a sign that said: "Call Heaven, speak with God, $.25." The young salesman did his business with the owner, all the while glancing at the phone. When finished he finally commented, "I've been all over the country, few countries overseas even and I have seen a few of these phones around but they all say that you can call Heaven and speak with God but the charge is always $100.00 yet here in this little village I see the same phone with the same message but the price is only $.25, how is that possible?" Marv Swing looked at him for a few seconds, smiled his friendly, small-town smile and said, "Son, you're in Fountain Creek, Heaven's just a local call from here."

I will leave you with one slow, soft, warm picture to fill your mind, your heart and your memory and stoke the "home fires" which may be burning in your heart for the better days we all remember. In the winter, a few weeks before Christmas, Swing Elevator in Fountain Creek would open a burlap bag in the middle of the floor, near the oil heater supplying the warmth to the office building. It was a 100 lb. bag of peanuts. Some of the farmers would be in the elevator taking care of business, and some if not most, would be there because this was their social center. This is where the men of the neighborhood, the men from the surrounding farms, would come to discuss Friday night's high school basketball game, the weather, last fall's harvest, next year's new seed numbers, the upcoming holidays, new equipment on the market and any and everything worth discussing. They would grab a handful of peanuts from the bag, sit down, and visit, everyone on an even level: farmers, businessmen, and pillars of the community, friends and neighbors all. As they talked, told jokes, shared the good and the bad, shared the laughter and sometimes even the tears, they shelled the peanuts and dropped the shells on the old hardwood floor in the office. As they got up, moved around, came and went, they ground the shells on the floor, and the old hardwood floor was treated to the best possible conditioning a hardwood floor could get; peanut oil. When the first bag was finished there would be another, and the coffee, friendship, peanuts, laughter, and sadness continued for most of the winter months. As this picture fades from my mind I still see them sitting in the office with their cups of coffee and a few peanuts, and to this day, I can still hear and recognize the voice and the laughter of Marv Swing, Dwight Leigh, Herman Bauer, Lawrence Leigh, Ray Eisenmann, Elmer Bauer, Harry Hoffman, Walt Johnson, Will Gudeman, Andy Bauer, Otto Knoll, Kenneth Hammerton, Clarence Baker, Glenn Strom, Fred Stock and so many more. All memories now, all gone on to glory and I miss them, but there is still my Fountain Creek, standing strong. Memories of sadness, happiness, a great childhood in a great place to have been a child, and yet there she is, strong as ever. I miss those days and that place, as do so many of you, with your own memories of your own Fountain Creek. No matter where I may roam, or where I may live, my heart will always be in Fountain Creek. Yes, you may take the boy out of Fountain Creek, but you can never take Fountain Creek out of the boy. World War II didn't diminish the light in my father's memory and as I grow older, the years I have spent gone from there while in the military, overseas, all the towns and cities I have been in have not diminished the light of Fountain Creek in my mind either. I miss my Fountain Creek and nothing can or will ever replace her.

God Finds Us

You often hear someone say "You need to find God and get right with Him." They mean well when they say this, but this cannot happen. In the book of John, chapter 6, verse 44 it says, "No man can come to me, except the Father which has sent me draw him: and I will raise him up at the last day." This is very clear and easy to understand. We cannot find God. He finds us and calls us. If it were up to us humans, none of us would have ever been saved. There is something in every human that would have prevented us from finding God on our own. In each one of us, some deeper than others, there is that which makes us think we are right. We know the answer and we have figured it out. None of us would have searched out God on our own. We would never have searched for someone who would tell us that we don't know all the answers and that we are not in charge of our own destiny. We don't find God; we don't even look for Him. He finds us. He does give us the "free will" to choose whether we will accept His calling or not, but He does the calling. There is nothing we can do to help ourselves. Ephesians chapter 2, verses 8 and 9 say it even more clearly, and also give us the reason. "For by grace are ye saved through faith; and that not of yourselves: it is the gift of God: Not of works lest any man should boast." We have nothing to do with being called. All we need do is accept the free gift of salvation.

I like the book of Luke. Luke was an educated man and pays a lot of attention to the details which are sometimes not in the other three gospels. The book of John is one of the first books a new convert should read, very good book, but I like the details in Luke.

At the 3rd hour they lead Jesus and the "two others" to be crucified to Calvary, or in the Hebrew tongue, "Golgotha," the place of the skull. Crucifixion was one of the most painful, inhuman ways ever devised to put a person to death. As they hung on the cross it was almost impossible to draw in a full breath of air and basically a man suffered a slow, painful, miserable death; basically smothering as he hung there. To get a good breath of air they had to push up with their feet, giving them room to inhale. This is the reason that the Roman soldiers would break their legs if they lived too long. With their legs broken they could not lift themselves up to breath, thus hastening their death. Jesus' cross was placed in the middle, between the two criminals who were crucified with him. Three of the four gospels tell of the comments made by the onlookers and the criminals on the cross, chiding Jesus. Crucifixion was reserved for the worst of the worst. These two who were crucified with Jesus were obviously hardened criminals, with very few, if any redeeming qualities. At some point in time, during all the comments, God found one of them and called him. I don't know when, what was said, or how it was done, but obviously the Holy Spirit moved into his heart and convicted him of his sin. As the other "malefactor" said to Jesus, "If thou be Christ, save thyself and us," the other, the one in whom the Holy Spirit had moved rebuked him saying, "Dost not thou fear God, seeing thou art in the same condemnation? And we indeed justly; for we receive the due rewards of our deeds: but this man has done nothing amiss." And he said unto Jesus, "Lord, remember me when thou comest into thy kingdom." And Jesus said unto him, "Verily I say unto thee, To day shalt thou be with me in paradise." What an amazing testimony of God's faithfulness and power. This man had lived a life of crime; I don't know what all he had done, but here, in this short amount of time, he was called, heard God, and answered. If I may paraphrase Dr. Spurgeon I believe it was: "This man had breakfast on earth with the devil, and supper in Heaven with the Lord." In a matter of a few short hours he went from "hell-bound" to "Heaven-found." He did nothing to deserve this, God found him. Just as you and I have done nothing to deserve our salvation, God found us. He lived during the time and life of Jesus and may have never heard of Jesus, I don't know, but I do know that when he was facing death he heard the Lord call and he accepted the gift and is now in Heaven with Jesus. Somewhere between the 3rd hour and the 6th hour of the day of his death He accepted the salvation that Jesus was finishing on the cross. We know that this man was saved from eternal damnation because the Bible says so; because he knew of the holiness of Jesus, and there was only one way he could have known that: God called him, the Holy Spirit convicted him, and Jesus saved him.

There is one other that we don't know for sure about. The Bible isn't as clear about his future and his salvation as the criminal on the cross. There was a Roman centurion assigned to watch the crucifixion, to ensure it was done correctly, and completely, and that the three being crucified did indeed actually die. This man was the cream of the crop in the Roman army. He; either by political appointment, or most probably by distinguishing himself in combat as a brave, honorable soldier who did as he was told, had earned the rank of centurion. He was over one hundred other Roman soldiers. He had very probably taken many lives, and had no problem with another. He did as he was told, when he was told, and had no problem with the orders he was given and that he followed. In the book of Mark we are told that after Jesus said, "It is finished," referring to the work of salvation, which He had finished, completed, and paid for in full, that He cried with a loud voice and gave up the ghost. "And when the centurion, which stood over against him, saw that he so cried out, and gave up the ghost, he said, Truly this man was the Son of God." We hear nothing more about the centurion in any of the scriptures, but I believe that at that moment he also was saved. I apologize, I am not adding to the words of the Bible, and I don't know, nobody knows except God and the centurion, but he knew that Jesus was the Son of God, and I believe he also was saved that day. I doubt very much if he was of much use to the Roman army after that revelation that day. When you look upon the face of God somehow I don't think you are ever the same. He had probably lost the taste for being the good soldier that he had obviously been to have been promoted to centurion.

I am not here as a judge of that, it is not my intention and something I have no way of knowing, but what I am saying is that God, in His magnificent wisdom calls whom He will call, when He will call them, and that is His right and His honor and His glory. There is nothing we can do to save ourselves, nothing we can say to save ourselves: we are called by God at His perfect time, in His perfect way, and He will call whom He will call.

Jesus didn't have to go to the cross: He was perfect and had never sinned; there was no reason for Him to go to the cross: but He went. At the 3rd hour he was nailed to my cross, bearing my sins and all the sins of the world, and hung up to die. He could have come down from the cross at any time for He is God and He can do anything; but He chose to stay on the cross. He was surrounded by angels; the very angels He had created and who, ever since their creation had served, praised and honored Him as their Lord and Master. They begged Jesus to let them save him, but He told them that this was why He had come into this world. They sheathed their swords and watched as their Lord and Master hung on the cross, bearing the righteous wrath of God for all we who actually deserved what Jesus was going through for us. Jesus traded his perfect life for our sin-filled lives. He who had never sinned became sin for us that we might live. We deserve the wrath of God which He endured. I deserved the beating and the crucifixion and the death which Jesus endured, but He knew I couldn't take it and could not pay my own ransom, so Jesus took my place and as God the Father looks at me now He sees Jesus on the cross paying my ransom. As He looked at His Son on the cross He saw me receiving what I deserved and I am justified because of the righteousness of Jesus. We don't find God; He finds us and I for one am glad because on my own I would never have found Him and by the grace of God I am saved. Mercy is when we don't get what we deserve, and grace is when we get what we don't deserve. Thank God that He is a loving God of mercy and grace.

For God so loved the world, that he gave his only begotten Son, that whosoever believeth in him shall not perish, but have everlasting life. For God sent not his Son into the world to condemn the world; but that the world through him might be saved. John 3:16, 17

GOD NEVER LEAVES ...

... and after Jesus arose from the grave, defeating sin, death and the devil, completely, He walked this world, teaching, preaching and testifying. He was witnessed by over five hundred people; witnesses who could and would testify that this was indeed He who died on the cross, was buried and rose again on the third day. His brow bore the scars of the crown of thorns, his back bore the scars of the scourging, his side bore the scar of the spear thrust in him as He hung on the cross, and his hands and feet bore the scars of the nails which held Him on the cross. After forty days he ascended into Heaven, His rightful home, the Heaven which He himself had created, where He lived with God the Father. Before He left this earth, He said that The Father would not leave us alone, but would send a helper, a comforter... AND HE DID!

God the Father, Jehovah, and God the Son, Jesus Christ, sit on their respectful thrones in Heaven. God the Father sits in the center of Heaven, the center of all creation, on the Great White Throne, the throne of God Almighty. God the Son, Jesus Christ, the God of my creation and the God of my salvation, sits on the throne of the King, to the immediate right of the Great White Throne, and they see everything I do, hear everything I say, know everything I think, and know what I do that I should not do, and what I don't do that I should do. God the Holy Spirit, the third part of the Holy Trinity was sent down to earth to live within me, in my soul, as Jesus said the Father would do. God the Father, God the Son, and God the Holy Spirit; three in one, all the same, all God, identical in thought, power, grace and mercy. The Holy Spirit knows me, intimately, and everything about me. I prayed for wisdom, that I might make my Father happy, that He might answer His critics, and He gave me all the wisdom of the ages; His wisdom in me, through the Holy Spirit. He gave me the knowledge to use the wisdom correctly, but so often I fail to use the wisdom correctly because I do not follow Jesus' examples, and wait on the Lord for his guidance, help, strength and power. When thoughts of sin enter my mind, and sin enters my body, I act, or react, and I sin against my God. The Holy Spirit, knowing me intimately and everything about me, sees and knows instantly, and my sin grieves the Holy Spirit. My sin grieves my Lord and my God. My sin shames me: that I would sin against my God. My God who created me, sent His Son to take my sin upon His perfect body and take my place on my cross, bearing my sin, and die my death and pay my debt, forever. My Savior who bore the "wrath of God" because He knew I couldn't. How could I sin against my perfect God, who would do this for me? My sin grieves the Holy Spirit and shames me.

… but the Holy Spirit knows me so well that He knows instantly what I am thinking and immediately calls upon God the Father in Heaven, who immediately hears and answers the Holy Spirit. When the Holy Spirit calls upon God the Father, the Father knows that His son is in trouble and no matter how busy in Heaven, or how busy elsewhere on earth, God the Father comes down from Heaven instantly to save His son. God the Father takes the load of sin off me that I had no business taking on me, and He pulls me from the filth and slime where sin always drives me and He forgives my sin and cleanses me again, making me pure and holy again before Him. He then takes me to the "high" road, the "straight and narrow" road where God walks, and He lets me walk beside him. I get so close to Him that I can feel His warmth, His strength, His mercy, His love, and I feel His arm upon my back and His hand on my shoulder as He lets me walk alongside Him as a loving father walks alongside his son. As we walk we visit. He talks to me and tells me things and shows me things and He hears every word I say to Him. He allows me to pray to Him. The Almighty God allows me, who was once the chiefest of sinners, and am now a son of God, to pray to Him. He hears every plea, prayer and petition, and He answers my every asking. Jesus said that whatsoever we ask in faith, in the name of Jesus, shall be granted, and my Lord has never lied to me yet and He never will. It is impossible for God to tell a lie, we may rest assured that every promise of the Lord is true and will be honored. God cannot lie, has never made a mistake, and is always true, pure and perfect.

… and as I walk by my Father, and we visit, I am in the most comfortable, safe, loving and cared for state of my being. Peter, James and John had the mountaintop experience with Jesus and wanted to stay there, on the mountain forever. Jesus told them they could not, but had to return to the world. My walk with my Heavenly Father isn't a mountaintop experience, but rather reality. God allows me to pray to Him, and allows me the closeness because He loves me, unconditionally. His love never varies. He never leaves; it is I who leave Him. So often we hear Adam and Eve condemned because they walked and talked with God in the Garden of Eden, and yet gave in to sin and sinned against their Father. That is no different than I. I walk and talk with God, on the "high" road, and yet, being a weak human, who too often has too weak a faith, and I begin to slip away. The thoughts of sin enter my mind, sin enters my body, and I begin to pull away from my Father, and I feel His arm slipping from my back, His hand slipping from my shoulder, and as I step off the smooth road, and onto the rocky shoulder of the road, I stumble and slip, and yet I do not go back to the comfort, safe zone, but continue in sin, and I leave my "Garden of Eden" and I fail, again.

… but the Holy Spirit knows me so well that He knows instantly what I am thinking and immediately calls upon God the Father in Heaven, who immediately hears and answers the Holy Spirit. When the Holy Spirit calls upon God the Father, the Father knows that His son is in trouble and no matter how busy in Heaven, or how busy elsewhere on earth, God the Father comes down from Heaven instantly to save His son. God the Father takes the load of sin off me that I had no business taking on me, and pulls me from the filth and slime where sin always drives me and He forgives my sin and cleanses me again, making me pure and holy again before Him. He then takes me to the "high" road, the "straight and narrow" road where God walks, and He lets me walk beside him, again. God never changes and He welcomes me back into the fold as though I had never left. God is a God of love and mercy and kindness and He always welcomes me back when I come to him in repentance and ask His forgiveness. My God is perfect and he doesn't live to condemn, but rather to restore.

We don't "find" God! He "finds" us, always, and He never leaves us. After I sin and pull away, God will still forgive my sins and take me back and love me as though my sins never happened. Jesus died and paid for all of my sins, every one, so God doesn't hold them against me. He removes them as far from me as the east is from the west and He chooses to remember them no more. He never revisits them upon me and never judges me with them. God is a merciful God of "2nd" chances, and I can't begin to count the "2nd" chances He has given me. My God never changes and never leaves. I am the one who puts distance between God and me, and when I pray to my Father for forgiveness, He forgives my sins, removes them, and closes the distance that I created. When Jesus died my death on my cross and paid my debt, He paid for all of my sins; past, present and future. I can do nothing about the past sins, I have repented of them and have been forgiven for them, but I shudder with shame that there are still present and future sins. How could I sin against this perfect God, who has promised me eternal life in Heaven and has given His "perfect" life for my "sin-filled" life? ... but I know that my God, my Heavenly Father, loves me unconditionally, forgives my sins, and chooses to remember them no more, and that I am an adopted son of God, a joint heir of Heaven with Jesus Christ, God's only begotten son, and that in the "Book of Life" in Heaven, on a page, written in God's beautiful, perfect hand writing is my name. God the Father, God the Son, and God the Holy Spirit, the God of my creation and the God of my Salvation is everything to me and all I will ever need. Praise be to God! Only He is worthy of all praise and honor!

For I know whom I have believed, and am persuaded that He is able, to keep that which I've committed unto Him against that day ...

God's Throne Room

I walked slowly down the huge, magnificent hallway, turning my head, trying to take it all in. The floor upon which I walked was solid gold; beaten to a beautiful shine and finish and sparkling, almost transparent, as were the walls, and the ceiling so high above me. I was walking towards the open door at the end of the hallway. I passed door openings in the hallway, marveling that none of them had a door attached. There was not a single, closed door in Heaven: in fact there was not a single door in Heaven, just the openings in the walls, and room after room of solid gold, as the hallway I was walking. The light was brilliant, and yet you could see everything, no squinting, no shadows, nothing to block the view. As bright as it was in the hallway, nothing compared to the light in the opening at the end of the hall where I was heading. As I walked the hall, I saw reflections of myself in the gold of the walls and the floor and no mirror has ever been clearer.

I stopped a few feet inside the door at the end of the hall. The first thing I saw when I entered the room was He who sat on the "Great White Throne" and He sparkled like jasper, glory shining from him like the facets of a diamond turning in a bright light and I knew instantly that I had entered the great throne room of the King. To

His immediate right I saw my Lord and Savior, Jesus Christ, the risen Son of the Living God, seated on His throne. As far as I could see to the left and to the right and behind the throne were angels: ten thousands times ten thousands, as far as the eye could see. All magnificent in the robes so pure white that they shined in the light of the Glory of God: the angels all created to serve and to glorify God, messengers of the Lord. I started to walk, slowly again, towards the throne of God, my God. As I approached the throne an angel stepped out from the multitudes, turned and bowed towards the throne, turned towards me, drew his sword, and approached me.

"Who are you and where do you think you are going?" he asked. I lowered my head and said, "I am sorry Sir, but my name is Roger and I am going to the throne of God." He almost laughed at what he must have considered my terrible arrogance. "Look at you" he said. "All around you is pure beauty; shining gold, the glory of God, angels dressed in white, nothing but purity, and you dare approach the throne of God looking the way you do?" "Again I am sorry Sir, for I have seen my reflection in the magnificent walls, and I know that I do not approach the beauty that is before me. I am old, tired, slow, and worn-out, my hair, what there is left of it has turned gray, my face is old and weathered, wrinkled like leather that has spent too many days in the hot sun and then in the cold of winter. My eyesight and my hearing are both failing; not nearly as good as they were when I was a younger man. The skin on my arms is scarred, discolored, and spotted and my arms are weakening. My hands are calloused from too many years of labor, my fingers stiff and sore from age and abuse. My legs are weakening and my knees fail me often and I stumble as I walk. My clothes are old and worn and faded from being worn too often and washed too many times. I know that compared to the beauty that surrounds me, I am not pleasing to look at but I do not believe God judges by the external appearance, but rather by the internal integrity. I do not even come close to fitting in the way I look but I don't believe God would exclude me because I am getting old and worn out."

"Well," continued the angel, "if you can look like that and still feel justified in approaching the throne of God you must be someone very special who has done some great thing or great and noble things to warrant passage. What have you done with your life for which God himself needs to honor you?" "Oh no Sir," I replied, "quite the opposite." "I am one who fought against God for a long time. I was born a sinner and for years I did all I could to be even worse. I am the chief of all sinners. I have done things to God that would shame even the demons. I know angels such as you could not even comprehend some of the terrible injustices I have been involved in. God gave me a talent and I turned my back on it and on Him. I abused my talent so badly that God took it back away from me, never to be mine again, never to be offered to me again. I have shunned him so many times. I have shamed and embarrassed God on so many occasions, and yet, yes, I am going to the throne of God."

"You agree that you look terrible, not good enough to present yourself at the throne, and you agree that you are a terrible sinner and have done nothing for God, and yet you persist in attempting to visit the throne" the angel said. "What gives you the right to approach the throne of God?" he asked. At that question I finally lifted my head, smiled and even found a little more strength for my voice. "I wish you would have asked that in the first place," I said to the angel. "This question I can answer. I have told you all the bad of my life, but there is also this: while all the terrible, filthy sinning was going on in my life I was told about Jesus Christ, the Son of God, who died for me. Ever since before time God has known me and knew that I was completely lost and unsaveable on my own, and He had a plan even then for me. At the correct time in His plan, His only begotten

Son, Jesus was born to a woman on earth. He was the Son of God, but also the Son of Man. He lived a perfect life on earth and when His time was about finished here, rather than going back to Heaven to claim His crown and throne, he stayed on earth to do what the Father had sent Him to do: He died for me. He was captured, put on trial, condemned to death by crucifixion, stripped, whipped, beaten, ridiculed, a crown of thorns beat down on His head with a stick, and all the while he uttered not a sound. This was all what I had deserved, and the punishment that should have been mine, but God took it away from me and let His own son take it in my place. After all this, they took Him out to a place on the side of the road called Golgotha, the place of the skull, and there they nailed Him to a cross and hung him between Heaven and earth and watched to see Him die. All of this I found out years later, but I now know the truth. As Jesus hung on the cross, the Roman soldiers took a spear and stabbed him in the side and his 'blood flowed like water' down His body, down the trunk of the cross, and down through the ages to me, covering my soul with His blood. Jesus opened the door to Heaven for me and paid the price for my salvation. I didn't have to do a thing except accept what had already been done and what had already been given. When I realized my sin and knocked on Heaven's door, God himself answered the door and bid me enter. He said he had been waiting for me. I repented of my sins and God took them from me and moved them as far from me as the east is from the west, and He chooses to remember them no more. I know me and what sin I am, but God knows me even better and as He looked into me at what I know to be my shriveled, ugly, blackened soul, He saw only a beautiful, snow white soul, covered with the crimson blood of His son. God forgave me of my sins and asked me to call Him my Father; no, rather, Abba Father. I told you I look terrible, old and worn-out, that I was a terrible sinner and shamed my God, but you finally asked me what gave me the right to approach the throne of God. GOD himself gave me that right, He told me to 'boldly go before the throne.' What gives me the right to approach the throne of God: I am a child of the King… I am a child of God… He is my father… I am a Son of God. I am HIS son…"

As I finished speaking the angel noticed tears flowing from my eyes. "Why do you cry, I should think you would be very happy?" "Oh, I am very happy to be the son of God, very happy, but as I was speaking I looked at Jesus, my Redeemer, and He smiled at me, which brings back the pain and shame I feel when I remember my responsibility for the 'man-made' things in Heaven." "Man-made things in Heaven?" he questioned, "Heaven was made by the spoken word of God, no part of Heaven is man-made, it is all 'God-made." "No Sir, I didn't say part of Heaven was 'man-made,' I said some 'things' in Heaven were 'man-made." "You see, when they captured Jesus and held his trial which was nothing but a mockery, they beat a crown of thorns down on Jesus' head, which left scars on his brow; and when they stripped him and whipped him with their whip, it left terrible scars on Jesus' back, and when they nailed him to the cross it left scars on his hands and feet, and when they stabbed him with the spear as he hung on the cross it left a large scar on his side." "Jesus still bears these scars today, even here in Heaven." "I told you Jesus took my place." "These scars should all be mine, on my body; for they were for my sins He took them." "These scars are the only man-made things in Heaven, and they are because of me and will be my pain and shame until I die and get to come to Heaven for eternity, where there will no longer be any pain or sorrow." "The pain and humiliation which Jesus suffered lead to the scars He still wears, and I am responsible for the only man-made things in Heaven, and when I looked at Jesus now, He smiled at me … He smiled at me? … and you wonder why I cry?"

At this the angel turned to the throne of God, bowed low and slowly, turned to the throne of Jesus, bowed low and slowly and then turned back to me, with tears in his eyes, sheathed his sword, smiled, nodded his head and stepped back into the multitudes of angels. I then heard him say in the sweetest of voices, "Step forward son of God, boldly go before the throne, for your father awaits you. The throne of God, which is always available for a child of God and with joy He awaits your arrival."

What a day that shall be, when my Jesus I shall see, and I look upon His face, the one who saved my by His grace, and He takes me by the hand and leads me to the promised land, what a day, glorious day that shall be …

HEAVEN'S FLOWERS

A long time ago, when the earth was brand new, Adam and Eve lived in a Paradise here below.

Then one day, sin entered their lives, they were banished, with no place to go.

Our Father above, a God of Mercy, walked through Heaven's gardens of gold,

And picked precious flowers and sent them to earth for Adam and Eve to hold.

The flowers came in the form of children; it's still done the same way today,

When a new child is born, God still sends a flower to dwell in its heart for a day.

Now some people say that God would never treat a special flower that way;

Take it from Paradise and send it to earth, to live with sin for a day.

God knows we humans are always too busy to enjoy the wonders of earth,

So only the eyes of an innocent child can show you creations worth.

They're not ours to own, we only borrow, a child's spirit is controlled from above,

But isn't this world a better place to live because of the little eyes of love?

We're too busy to notice the world around us; we're far too busy to stop,

But to a child's eyes, this world's a Paradise that only Heaven can top.

So children were sent as little flowers, so we could appreciate our place,

No sight is as sacred as the sight of a smile, shining on our small child's face.

The rose on earth is a beautiful flower, no other flower on earth can compare,

But the smile on the face of a little child is far more beautiful, more fair.

So as it must happen, children grow older and soon sin enters their heart,

So the golden flower is spirited to Heaven to come back as another new start.

Then comes the day when they must decide, which force will rule their life,

Each child must answer on his own, Heaven's glory or Satan's strife.

Someday unawares, an Angel comes down and spirits the flower back above,

Where it will come, back down to earth, to replenish the world with love.

So the next time you look at a little child, look through different eyes,

You're not just seeing a little person; it's a golden flower, a prize.

When your little child says "I love you," his little smile shining like gold,

As a parent you'll whisper, with a tear in your eye, "Please God, don't make him grow old."

But as it must, the flower will leave, for Heaven's glory it must depart.

Now it's up to us, he belongs to the world; God has surely done his part.

When we get to Heaven, we'll walk the garden, the one where those little flowers grew,

We'll smile when we see, in our mind's eye the reflection, the faces of the children we knew.

While they're on earth they're ours to protect, we gather them into our fold,

And though we know better, you'll hear us whisper, "Please God, don't make him grow old."

Take heed that you despise not one of these little ones; for I say unto you, That in Heaven their angels do always behold the face of my Father which is in heaven.

Imagine

Imagine, if you would, it's the end of the day, you are home from work, sitting in your chair, relaxing, resting, and there is a knock at your door. You get up and answer it and there are two policemen there. You ask what you can do to help them and they ask to see your identification and upon looking at your driver's license they look at each other and one says, "Yes, it is him." They arrest you, take you into custody, place handcuffs on you, put you in the back seat of the police car and take you to jail where you are locked up. The following morning you are taken to a court room and await your turn before the judge. Finally your name is called, it is your turn, and you stand before the judge.

The judge asks what the charges are and a gentleman representing the court begins to read: murder, rape, stealing, lying, cheating, crooked business dealings, failure to report any and all income, not paying all taxes, and the list goes on. You stand there with your head bowed and realize that all being said is true. When the list is finally finished it is announced that these have been going on all of your life. There is an audible gasp and then quiet, finally, deafening quiet. You can't even lift your head to look at the judge who you realize by now is probably totally disgusted and sickened by what he has heard. When finally the judge speaks he simply asks; "how does the accused plead to these charges?" When you can finally speak around the lump in your throat and the shame of the reality of the charges, you raise your head, look at the judge and quietly say, "guilty your honor, guilty of each and every charge." He asks you again if you are guilty of all the charges and you pause and then say, "Yes your honor, all the charges, I am guilty." The judge then says that he has no choice but to accept your guilty plea and will now pass sentence. He says that because of the severity of the charges and the length of time they have been going on, all of your life, you are sentenced to death, and the sentence will be carried out immediately. As the judge finished passing sentence there is a small commotion behind you in the gallery and a voice is heard saying, "May I approach the bench your honor?" The judge asks the reason for the approach, and the voice says, "I am here to stand for the accused and to take his place." There is a loud gasp and much murmuring as the gallery realizes the man speaking is the son of the judge, his only son. He approaches the bench and stands before the judge, his father. The judge asks the meaning of this intrusion and the son responds that this is the reason for which he was born into this world. He knew this was going to happen and he was here to take your place. The judge says this is highly irregular, never having been done before, but he would grant his son his wish.

You stand there in awe as the shackles are removed from you and placed on the judge's son, and the paperwork is all changed, with all of your charges being put on another sheet of paper with the judge's son's name on it, and all the charges are put on him, to be carried out as they were to be carried out on you just a short time earlier, his sentence now is death, immediately,

as it was to be for you. You stand there as the judge signs the death sentence for his own son. The accused is now escorted out to the courtyard where the sentence will be carried out, and you are told to accompany him to witness the proceedings. The judge will not accompany the accused, even though it is his own son. As a judge he is sworn to uphold the law and be no part of anything illegal or immoral and the death of his son for these charges certainly falls under the illegal and immoral clause, and he refuses to accompany his own son, to uphold the integrity of the court. You stand and watch, with the most accusing, burning, aching in your heart that you can ever imagine, even though the proceedings mean your eventual freedom. You watch as the judge's son, with your charges and sins on his body, is put to your death, paying your debt, and you watch until he is pronounced dead.

You are taken back into the courtroom afterwards and the judge is still sitting at the bench, and when you enter the room he hands you the sheet of paper with all of your charges on it, and it is also stamped "Paid in Full." He tells you that you are free to go, never again to be charged with any of these crimes as they have been paid and will never be brought up again. You ask how this can be, you have done nothing to warrant this, absolutely nothing to win your freedom and the judge says, "You are right, you have done nothing to win your freedom, you have done nothing to pay your debt, for there was nothing you could do. You were guilty, by your own admission, and death was the only sentence that could be passed down, and you, or someone in your place had to die. My son died for you, no, you did nothing at all to win your freedom or to deserve what has been done for you." Furthermore the judge tells you that because his son loved you enough to die for you that there is a reward awaiting you at some point in the future. A mansion, eternal happiness and joy, and a glorious forever await you, but he will not tell you when that will happen, but he does tell you that you will be blessed beyond your wildest imagination in the interim, just as a preview of the glory to come. You were guilty of all charges, completely, and his son paid your debt, and you are rewarded, eternally, because of what his son did for you, dying in your place.

I entitled this short story "Imagine" and the first word in the story is imagine, but that is sorely lacking. The title should have been "Believe" and the first word should have been believe. There is no imagine to this story, it is all true, told to you by me as it happened. The judge in the story is "God the Father." The man who died for the guilty charged criminal is "Jesus, God's only Son." The guilty accused in this story is me, and all of the charges against me are true. No, I did not physically kill anyone, I am not guilty of physical murder, but I have hated and the Bible says that to hate someone is to have murdered him. I have not physically raped any women, but I have been guilty of lust and that is the same as having performed the act. Sadly enough, all of the rest of the charges listed are true and I have broken probably every law against God and man, but, I who was once the chiefest of all sinners, the most despicable of all men, am now a son of God, and promised eternal life in Heaven because Jesus, the Son of God, loved me enough to take my sin on himself, take my place, on my cross, die my death, and pay my debt in full. I who am the least deserving am promised eternity in Heaven with my Lord, where I will never again shame my Father, never again sin, and finally be a perfect Son of God. I will finally be one with the Son as the Son is one with the Father. I who was once the worst of sinners am now a joint heir of Heaven with Jesus, the Risen Son of the Living Father. I have played absolutely no part in my own salvation; it was all done by Jesus, for me, the undeserving. Praise God!

A dear friend of mine asked me recently why nobody had ever seen the kind, caring, decent side of me before. After much thought, and praying about it, I realized that there is no kind, caring, decent side of me to be seen. I was the worst of sinners, and now, by the Grace of

God, I am a son of God, and because of His mercy, I shall live with Him forever. Maybe He will allow me to tell my story, and other stories to help others see that there is a good, great, and glorious, awaiting all of us if we but accept what Jesus has done for us. We can do nothing to warrant any of this. Jesus has already done it all. It is finished, completed, because He loves us in spite of what we are and in spite of what we have done. As Jesus said from the cross, just before dying ….. "It is finished….."

... In My Stead

It was cold, windy and raining that morning, only a half hour after sunrise, as I walked down the city street. I was already cold and wet, both from the rain and the cars passing by, splashing me as they drove through the puddles on the street, in a bad mood from being hungry, wet, and disappointed in everything associated with my life so far. Here it was, so early in the morning and I already had enough. I had no place to go and all day to get there, nothing to do and an entire lifetime to do it. Something had to go right at some point in time didn't it? How much was I supposed to take? Give me a break. I had been walking with my head down and my hood up trying to keep at least part of me dry. I stopped at an intersection and looked around to get my bearings. I had stopped in front of a large church on the corner, and as I looked at it, my mind was flooded with memories, memories of my youth, when our folks would take us to church on Sunday. I remembered the feelings of comfort, warmth, and of belonging that were associated with the time I spent in church and I wondered if I could sneak in the back and maybe get a little dry and warm before someone discovered me in my worn and torn clothes and asked me to leave. I finally walked up the few steps, took hold of the large wooden door and it silently, smoothly opened and I walked in. The door closed behind me and instantly I felt the warmth and the same feeling of belonging. I took my jacket off and put it over a heat vent on the floor. It was too dirty, and worn to hang on the coat rack where the decent people put their coats and hats.

Yeah, this felt good, the warmth was seeping into me slowly and it felt good to be in out of the rain. I wanted to pretend I belonged so I walked around the vestibule, read the bulletin board, read the names of the ladies who were in charge of the gift packages going overseas, pretended I knew them, a thank-you note from the disabled veterans for the donated quilts, and noticed that the church chili supper was this coming Saturday evening. "Bring sandwiches or your favorite pot of chili to be shared with the entire congregation." I pretended I belonged there and thought that would be good, I would enjoy that. I didn't have any sandwiches or chili and I had no way to get any, had no decent clothes to wear anyway, but it felt good to pretend that I was supposed to be there and I would be there with my friends on Saturday evening to enjoy the fellowship. I walked over and checked, my jacket was getting dry and was warm but not quite yet was I ready to leave, this felt good. I walked past the opened doors that lead to the sanctuary and looked inside. The room was still dark, except for one small light on a table in the front. I stepped inside and looked around. Nobody there to ask me to leave, nobody there to tell me I didn't belong, nobody there to tell me I was too dirty, so I walked towards the front of the church. I felt compelled to go to the small table with the light, I wanted to see it, and somehow I knew it had something for me.

We have all heard the stories about soldiers in combat. How one would give his life to save his fellow soldiers, his comrades, by falling on a live grenade or jumping in front of a friend to take the bullet for him. Yeah, I had heard the stories also, but couldn't bring myself to believe in that level of love, or integrity, or nobility. Nobody would do that. As I reached the small table I realized it was actually an alter, inscribed, and as I read it I realized it was a memorial, a tribute to the man, the soldier, who had given his own life in combat for mine. I read the inscription several times with tears welling up in my eyes and a terrible lump forming in my throat. The sadness and sorrow overtook me and tears ran down my face as I remembered the battles, the fighting, the sorrow, and the overwhelming sadness of losing yet again, another failure. It seemed the battles had lasted forever, each one worse than the one before, and always another to follow.

After several minutes I felt a presence beside me. I couldn't bring myself to look at someone, looking as badly as I did, sobbing, with tears streaming down my face and a lump in my throat too big to talk around anyway. I felt his strong, gentle hand as he placed it on my shoulder, his strong arm on my back, and somehow, instantly I knew who he was. He said nothing, just stood beside me, holding me as I cried. Finally I regained some of my composure. "I'm Roger, mine was the life that was saved by your son's sacrifice, which cost him his life." In a strong, soft voice I heard him say, "I know, I have always known. I have come here every day, always, ever since the day he died in your stead, knowing that some day you would come and I had to be here for you, as my son was there for you." As his son was there for me, that comment brought back even more, stronger memories. "He was always there, always. He never left me, not once, not for a second. No matter how hard or ugly the battle, he stayed, always there to help me, always there to do what needed doing and just always there. We went through so many life-shattering experiences, lost so many battles, defeated at every turn, my life a complete and utter failure, doomed, no, sentenced to die, and he never left me. I remember, finally, the last day, when there was just nothing left to do but let it be finished. I was done and could see no way out. I was hated by the enemy, they wanted my destruction, but your son would not let them get to me, but we reached the point where even he couldn't keep them away, so in my stead, he gave himself up to them. They beat him with their fists, stripped him and whipped him until his back was raw and bleeding. At one time, while this was going on I heard him say "Father, forgive them for they know not what they do." Doing this to him and he asked for you to forgive them? He should have hated me, not them, I put him in that place. They abused him until you could hardly recognize him as a man, and then they killed him. Right before he died I saw him raise his head, his eyes, and heard him say, "it is finished." I was forced to watch all of this, since he had gone in my stead. I never understood how he could do that for me. Can you make me understand how he could do that for me?" He said, "It isn't your place to understand that, simple men cannot understand that, not now, not here, but someday you will see through the glass clearly and all will be understood, for now it is enough for you to accept." Yes, but when he made the comments, took the horrible abuse, and died in my stead, it was almost as though that had been his mission all along. "It was" he said softly, "He loved you that much."

He commented to me that he understood that my father had passed away. Yes, I said, that was true; he had passed a few years ago. He then changed my life when he said, "but you are still not alone. I love you; I have always loved you. I have adopted you as my son, my son adopted you as his brother, and we are now family, you are now my son, and I am now your father." I told him I had a book, actually several letters put together in a book fashion for easier reading. There were 66 letters, written by 40 good friends of him and his son, and in there it is mentioned several times that he had adopted me as his son. I told him I had read all the letters at least once and most of them many times and I had enjoyed all I had read and learned about both him and his son. As we talked I felt a burning desire to know him better and I felt a terrible heavy weight lifting off me and I knew that everything was now going to be okay. I had been forgiven, for everything. It was that simple. He loved me, his son loved me, his son died for me, and yet he loved me enough to adopt me as his son. I felt a happiness that I had never before felt.

I knew it was time to go, as comfortable as it was I couldn't "stay on the mountain" forever, I had to finish my life on earth. I looked down at the alter and read the inscription again, out loud this time: "Jesus Christ, the risen son of the living God." This man, this soldier, this Son of God, had gone to the cross and died for me, who had hung him on the cross. He knew me, knew how badly I looked, saw my clothes, my attitude, and yet loved me enough to die in my stead. I turned to walk back down the aisle and leave. The sanctuary was empty, as I knew it would be, or so I thought. I walked toward the doors with a joy and a lightness I had never felt before. As I approached the back, I noticed an elderly man sitting in the shadows in the back pew of the church, and as I got closer, he stood up and stepped out in the aisle. "Is there something I can do for you son?" he asked. "No, thanks a bunch though, I have been helped more than you can imagine," I said. He then asked me how I had gotten into the church. I told him that I had just pulled on the door and it had opened for me and I had come in. I apologized if I had done something wrong in coming in as I had. He said that was not a problem, this was "the Lord's house" and all are welcome. He told me he was the minister there in that church, and that every morning he arrived at seven o'clock to unlock the doors, turn on the lights and prepare to serve anyone the Lord sent his way. When he got there this morning the doors were locked as usual, he had to unlock them with the key to come in. When he got in he noticed my jacket lying on the floor so he looked in the sanctuary and he saw two figures in the front of the church, one obviously in pain and agony and the other holding him and offering comfort. He could hear two voices talking but they were too soft to understand. He said he didn't know what was happening but it was obvious it was something special, so he sat in the back pew and waited. He had not turned on any lights nor opened anything yet, knew it was just his plan, not the Lord's. He told me that if the door opened as easily as I said it did, and I had received as much help at the alter as I said I had, then that explained who the second figure was at the alter. He said the other figure had a soft, warm glow surrounding it and when I turned to come back out, the second figure had faded from view.

I apologized again if I had caused any problems, he assured me that I had not, and so I picked up my old, worn jacket and opened the door and walked out to face the rest of my life, which suddenly felt much better than it had before. I don't know why but running through my mind was the thought: "this is the day that the Lord has made, let us rejoice and be glad in it."

"There are many hills to climb upward, I often am longing for rest; but He who appoints me my pathways, knows just what is needful and best."

MIKE'S EASTER LILIES

Mike was a little different than everyone else in the neighborhood. It was a nice neighborhood where everyone got along well, stood outside and visited, most probably didn't even lock their doors when leaving for a short time. Mike wasn't like that, not at all. When he would come home in the evening he would drive past folks out in the yard visiting, standing at the community mailbox visiting; doing whatever, just being friendly. Not Mike, he wouldn't return their waves so most folks didn't bother waving at him anymore. He wouldn't respond when they said hello so most folks didn't speak to him anymore. He wouldn't show up at a block party so most didn't bother inviting him anymore. He was just a loner, unfriendly, and seemed to prefer it that way. Never did any harm to anyone; never threatened anyone, never a problem, just never a part of the neighborhood. Didn't seem to hate anyone, just didn't seem to want anyone to like him either.

He was a big man, stood about 6'4", and weighed probably around 250 or 260, all muscle. He worked construction, outside, 12 months out of the year so he had to be tough enough to take that and he appeared to be. Hair was always shaggy and needed cut or combed, usually about a 2 or 3 day growth of beard, had a few tattoos and body piercings, the company he worked for provided his uniforms but he was one of those who tore the sleeves off, partly so he had room for his big arms, but also so you could see the tattoos better. It seemed that intimidating appearance went along well with his less than pleasant demeanor and attitude. He had been known to spend a little time at a roadhouse down the street once in a while, drinking a bit more than he should. You could tell if he had been there or not because when he came home after staying there too long he would park his pickup outside the garage rather than pull it in. A few years back he had tried to pull it in and had taken out half the side of the garage. He didn't do that any longer, just left it outside till he could negotiate it better. Guess about the nicest thing you could say about him is that he was "pretty," pretty ugly and pretty apt to stay that way. He had a nice little house and a nice yard. No landscaping, no flowerbeds, nothing special, but he did seem to take care of the house and always mowed the yard and had it looking nice. Had an 8' diameter area about 10' out from the front door where he had an old dead tree removed about a week earlier. When they ground the stump out it had fluffed the ground up well and about half the ground was small wood chips, nice seed bed but not for Mike, he was going to sow grass there next spring so he could mow it again in the summer, no need for a flower bed. Seemed like being in construction had taught him the value of building well and caring for something, but hadn't taught him to go out of his way to make it a little prettier with flowers or something, just maintain what was there. Not much pride in him, but seemed to have the pride in things built. Most of the neighbors would probably not even have known his last name if it weren't for the article in the local paper about a month ago when he had saved another worker's life on the construction site when a cave-in had buried him. He would have suffocated if not for Mike's quick action and knowing what to do. In typical "Mike" fashion he didn't have much to say when the papers and television people tried to interview him. Don't think he even really liked the man he saved, just probably thought it part of his job. Don't get me wrong, Mike didn't hate anyone, just didn't like anyone either, preferred to go on about his business by himself. Everyone just called him "Big Mike" and let him go on about his business his own way.

Big Mike came home from work one day shortly after having the tree removed and there on the step outside the front door was a small brown paper bag with a note attached. One of those days when Mike had to park in the driveway, so you know he was even less sociable than usual. Mike opened the bag, looked at the shriveled little round "whatevers" that were in the bag, and read the note which said, "Mike, thought you might like to plant these yet this fall, Bill." Mike didn't pay much attention to people around him but he did know that Bill was his next door neighbor. He looked again in the bag and actually got a bit mad at the contents. What's wrong with him anyway, giving me something old and dead like this and acting like it was something worth caring about and even planting, yeah right, I'll plant something that dead and ugly. Mike wasn't much on flowers and seeds and figured he was just being hassled. "Well, I'll show him what I think of this just in case he is watching out of his window" Mike thought as he walked out to the area where the tree had been removed. He opened the bag and scattered the seeds all over the dirt, wadded up the bag and the note and walked inside. Poor old Mike had no idea what he had just done. Came up a pretty big storm that evening, nice rain, drove the bulbs down into the dirt pretty well, then fall arrived pretty strong and the leaves blew down, blew around and quite a few settled over the dirt area, fall rains continued to soak the leaves and pack them down, making a pretty good mulch out of the wood shavings from the stump grinder mixing with the leaves. Pretty soon winter came along, snow fell, settled on it, did its job of protecting the seed bed. Sometimes the winters in Michigan can get tough and seem awfully long, but eventually winter ended and spring arrived.

Nobody knew what the problem was; Mike seemed even uglier than usual that spring, when you would have thought a construction worker would have been happy, warm weather coming would make the work so much easier. Whenever Mike had to park in the driveway he would walk in the front door and one day he saw these little shoots growing up out of the leaves and mulch on the area in his front yard. No idea what they were but even they make him mad, he had wanted to clean that up and sow grass but he just hadn't gotten around to it and now look, something growing there. Seemed like every time he saw them they were growing and unrolling and forming some sort of bud on the top of the stems. Then one day Mike came home, slow and quiet, parked the truck but something was different. He had not been drinking, just deep in some thoughts which seemed to be really tearing him up. As he walked to the front door he noticed the shoots that had grown. On top of them were the prettiest blossoms he had ever seen and as he stood there dumbfounded looking at such beauty, something came over him and he began to weep. Tears rolling down that big, tough, weathered, stubbly face. Bill, from next door, had just gone to get his mail and walked by and noticed this. He quietly walked up behind Mike and put his left hand on Mike's right shoulder and just stood there, tears rolling down his own face. Mike stood there shaking as he quietly sobbed for a few minutes more, then turned around and looked at Bill. He told Bill that he had just come from his doctor, where he had been told that he had cancer and that it was probably terminal, but he had to go back in two weeks from now for the rest of the tests and to be told what they were going to try to do for him. The combination of hearing of his impending death and coming home to see the prettiest flowers he had ever seen had been too much for him and he had just lost it, right there. He asked Bill who else had been there a few minutes earlier. Bill assured him that he was the only one there. Mike said that at the same time he felt Bill's hand on his right shoulder, he also felt a hand rest on his left shoulder. Bill just smiled through his tears. Mike then said he didn't know what had happened, but when he saw the flowers he just lost it. Said his whole life, as rotten as he had been, had passed through his mind and he realized how badly he had been treating people. Said he had never felt so alone and as ashamed of himself as he did right then. He didn't know what had happened. Mike asked what those flowers were and Bill told him they were known as Easter Lilies. Mike then asked a few questions quickly, not waiting for an answer. Who had put their hand on his other shoulder, why was Bill crying also, what is so special about the lilies, why did Bill even care? When he finally stopped talking, pausing to take a breath, he looked at Bill. Bill started slowly, weighing his words, not wanting to stop Mike's sudden interest in being human. He said, "Mike, I am a preacher at the church just two blocks down the street, and I was crying because in the Bible, in Romans, chapter 12 it says we should weep with those who weep. In Proverbs it says we should do our neighbors no harm because those who live next to us trust us. I care because the Bible also says that when we hurt, God hurts with us, and I couldn't stand to see you hurt so badly. I can't tell you what is so special about the Easter Lilies, but only what legend and tradition say. Tomorrow is Good Friday, making this Thursday. Legend has it that the night before he was crucified, Jesus was in the Garden of Gethsemane in such agony and praying so hard and sincere that he sweat drops of blood, and that those drops of sweat, and His tears, sprang up as the lilies you see before you. In the Bible Jesus is even referred to as the Lily of the Valley, so the lilies must be a very important, honored flower. The following day, after the night of agony in Gethsemane, Jesus was hung on a cross, where he took all the sins of the world, those from each and every one of us, onto his pure, perfect body, and He died so that we might live. I don't know what happened to you, nor do I know where the hand came from that settled on your left shoulder as I held your right one, but I would suspect that Jesus knew your pain and He visited you. He worked through the Holy Spirit to convict you and that is where your thoughts and tears came from, and I would even say that it may well have been the hand of Jesus you felt on your shoulder. I can't cure your cancer, but I can tell you who can, should He wish to. Tomorrow, as I said is Good Friday and Sunday is Easter Sunday. We are having services in church tomorrow evening at 7, and a sunrise service on Easter Sunday, where we begin at 7 in the morning with a breakfast and then a service in which we celebrate the day, the morning of the third day after his crucifixion, when Jesus came back to life and arose from the grave. I would like to invite you to both of those services should you like to come as a special friend and guest of mine." Mike said he would be there for both, as he had realized in the past few minutes that there were many people through the ages to whom he owed an apology, and that he believed he needed to learn more about, and speak with, Jesus. Said it was time he repented of his sins and joined the Lord's side.

Well, Mike showed up for both services, his hair cut and combed, clean clothes and even his boots polished. Sunday morning he walked down the aisle at the alter call, fell on his knees crying and accepted Jesus as his Savior. Bill presented him with a new Bible and Mike thanked him and said he would be reading it and coming over to speak with Bill whenever he needed help in understanding. Bill told him he was welcome anytime.

Postscript: Two weeks later, when Mike had to go for his tests and to speak with the doctor about any treatment which might help him, Bill stood at the window, watching and waiting for Mike to pull into his driveway, so he was surprised when he heard a knock at the door and he opened it to see Mike there smiling as big as Texas. He had parked in Bill's driveway instead of going to his own as he was in such a hurry to see Bill. Mike started talking, and as he spoke he got faster and louder he was so excited. "Bill, I owe this all to you and that small paper bag of seeds you left at my door. I think they are called bulbs, I'm not sure, but if you had not left them there, and I had not scattered them in the fresh dirt, and had the fall rains and the snow insulation not worked their magic in them, and had then not flowered right around Easter time, and had I not been given the bad news of my cancer, and had you not walked up behind me, and had you not known what to say and when to say it, I would have never come to know Jesus and I would not now be a saved Son of God, promised eternity in Heaven, the very Glory Jesus left when He came down to earth to die for my sins so that I might live forever. I have been reading the Bible, learning and enjoying it very much. You spoke of Proverbs so I read there quite often, and I learned that a close friend is better than a distant brother. That was you, a close friend as my two brothers are in Philadelphia where I was born. As you know, I saw the doctor today. He cannot explain what happened. He was all ready to treat me and figured that my cancer was terminal, and today he could find no trace of, nor evidence of, cancer, nor that I had ever had any problem. He presented me with a clean bill of health. I am certain beyond a shadow of a doubt that the hand on my left shoulder that day was the right hand of Jesus and that He healed me completely, before I even knew him. I have also read Chapter 12 in Romans, the one you used when you said we are to weep with those who weep. I read the rest of that verse, the part you skipped, and it also says we are to rejoice with those who rejoice. I would now ask you to rejoice with me, and I would appreciate it very much if you and your wife would accompany me to supper, to rejoice with your brother who rejoices in his healed soul, and his healed body, and is now ready to be a kind, friendly neighbor to all those around me in this neighborhood, all of those whom I have mistreated. I have many things to make right and it is about time to start. Come with me friend, my brother, and let's start rejoicing as God intends us to."

MY FATHER'S BROTHER

He was my father's oldest brother, and other than my own father, he was the greatest man I ever knew. My earliest recollection of him was on his farm. My grandfather was a farmer who had five sons. He must have had their love and respect because all five of his sons followed his example by becoming farmers themselves. As I said, my first memories of him are when he was on his farm. He and his wife raised six children of their own, four sons and two daughters. He was a man of many talents, but one of his greatest was his ability to work with wood. He could build anything; houses, a church, cabinets, furniture, frames, wooden toys, anything. I remember when he quit farming to go into construction completely. He and his sons as they grew into manhood built some of the most beautiful houses in the area. He also must have had his sons' love and respect because all four of them followed him into construction in one way or another, either with bricks and blocks, concrete, or became his partner in house construction as one did. If someone wanted a new house, remodeling, any building repaired or rebuilt, they called on him. I can recall many of the houses he built and most of them are as beautiful and as solid today as they were the day he finished building them. He took no shortcuts, nor would he short anyone on anything he was contracted to do. To be dishonest

72

just never occurred to him. He did his best, always, and was loved and respected by all for it. He was an honest man of integrity.

He was a big, strong man, as one would have expected being raised on a farm, working every day, then having his own farm, and then going into construction. He had an infectious smile and an easy way about him. I don't remember ever hearing him raise his voice, nor do I ever remember him being angry. His children may remember him differently at times as they grew into adulthood, but then it is supposed to be that way between a father and his children. Only they should know some things about their father, and they should never repeat most things. He was a minister, and a man of great convictions. Jesus said, "I am the way, the truth, and the life; no man cometh unto the Father but by me." My uncle believed this completely and he preached unashamedly and constantly that our only hope of salvation was the "shed blood of Jesus." There was no doubt, nor room for discussion, in his beliefs. Jesus was his Lord, his God, his Redeemer, his Heavenly Father, his strength, and his closest friend and companion. Wherever he went or whatever he did he was in constant communication with his Lord, and he was quite comfortable with the fact that his Lord was beside him constantly.

He had a strong love of music. I used to stand as close to him as I could when we were singing in church. He had a good, strong, bass voice and I loved to sing with him. I remember the Sunday I was trying so hard to sing with him when I realized that I was working myself hard to keep up with him and he wasn't trying anything extra, he was just singing normal, praising his Savior. He sang the hymns for the sheer pleasure of praising God. My father told me that when

they were kids my uncle played a pretty good harmonica. I never heard him play. I believe he played for his kids when they were growing up, probably for his grandchildren, but I never got to hear him play. When they were younger, growing up as a family back on the home farm, the boys all had pretty good, strong, singing voices and they would sing together, pretty good harmony, on occasion. My father told me that during the colder months they would sit in the living room in the farm house and their mother, my grandmother would ask them to sing for her. They would sing songs they knew from that era which they had heard on the radio or mostly the old gospel songs they learned in church every Sunday. When it was warmer, during the spring, summer and fall evenings they would sit on the porch on the west side of the house and sing. Depending upon which direction the wind was from, the neighbors on their farms could hear the boys singing and would often tell them or their father they next time they saw them. I believe all the boys kept their love for music throughout their lives.

My uncle had a love for classical, or symphony orchestra music. He had no formal musical training, but loved to direct the symphony as they played on the radio or the stereo. His kids used to tease him about that, but he loved the music, and continued to direct the orchestra.

When their kids were grown and gone, all very successful in their chosen careers, and life should have been a little easier and slower for them, when they should have had the time to appreciate each other finally after their years of hard work, life dealt them a hard, crushing, blow. His wife, the mother of his children, was stricken with a devastating disease which slowly destroyed the woman he loved. The Bible says we are "to love our wives as Christ loved the church." I believe he did in every sense of the word. He considered it his honor to care for her as best he could, and he was completely devoted to her care and welfare and comfort. Knowing some of the tests and trials he endured, I stand in awe of him. I never once heard an unkind word or complaint. She was his love, his wife, his partner, and she was his earthly joy. When he could no longer care for her alone because of age and her deteriorating health, I believe it hurt him deeply. I think he felt he was failing her. After she passed away, leaving him to join her Lord in Heaven, it was as though his reason to exist had gone. He spent his last few years in a home where he was cared for himself.

Towards the end of his life there were many times when even his kids didn't know whether he knew them or not as they would visit. When my own father passed away, one of his sons stopped to visit him in the home on his way to the visitation. He spoke with him, visiting as though his father heard and understood every work, not knowing whether or not his father even heard, let alone understood what he was saying. At one point in the conversation he leaned over towards his father and said, "Dad, Uncle Will passed away, we're going up to his visitation now." He continued to visit, but there, in his semi-conscious state, oblivious to what was going on around him, a tear formed in the corner of his father's eye. Even then, in that state, his love still showed through. He was a man among men on this earth. This is a better world because he was in it. He still lives on, through his children, grandchildren, and great-grandchildren. All of them are better people because of the example he set for so many in his life here on this earth.

I believe when I get to Heaven and am walking around at some point in time, I will hear harmonica music and when I follow the sound to the source, I will see my uncle sitting in the shade of the Tree of Life, maybe alone or maybe surrounded by his kids and their families, playing the old songs he remembers from his past. Maybe some of the old gospel hymns he and his brothers used to sing for their mother back here on earth years ago. I also fully expect to be there when he is invited to direct Heaven's symphony orchestra for a few of his old favorite songs. The training he didn't receive here on earth won't matter a bit there in Heaven, where all things will be made new and he will have all the training he will ever need. I believe the orchestra will sound very nice for those numbers he selects and chooses to lead.

He was my father's brother, and other than my own father, he was the one man I loved, respected and honored more than any other. He was a man of God and it was my thrill and my honor to have known him and a pleasure indeed to have learned so many things from the fine examples he set.

THE KING'S EXPRESS

There is an old abandoned railroad spur about 200 yards south of the farmstead where we have lived for the last several years. It was abandoned when we moved in so we have never seen a train run this line. Like a lot of old rail lines, it connected the small towns and handled mostly the grain from the grain elevators; moving the local farmers' grain harvest on to the world markets. I had walked the rails about a mile or two either way of the crossing and was always impressed; the line was in very good shape yet. Oh yes, the rails were rusty from years of no use and there were trees, shrubs and underbrush growing up on the entire right of way as well as between the rails. Would take a lot of cleaning up to make the line useable, but the rails were still straight and true, the ties were still solid, there were no washouts, the bridges still solid, all in all, still a very good, strong rail line. There was a small creek that ran under the tracks about fifty yards east of the road we lived on which had become a comfortable place for us through the years. Rather a romantic place, a few trees provided shade and an old tree stump just the right height to be a very comfortable seat, either for resting or for sitting and contemplating whatever was bothering you. As I said, it was quite comfortable and through the years we had several picnics in the area. Our oldest daughter's boyfriend had proposed marriage to her there on a Sunday afternoon following a picnic they had. I had become quite comfortable there when I had a problem or something that needed a lot of thought; good quiet place for thinking. Seemed close to God there. I felt like when I went there to talk to Him we were in one of His special places.

A few years back I was out behind the barn early one Saturday morning, repairing a door that had blown off during a spring storm. It was a nice warm summer day and I was enjoying just being there, not working too hard, answering to no one, building and hanging a barn door. I had been there about an hour and a half, just about finished when I felt the urge to go down to the tracks. As I said, a lazy day project, I was almost finished and what the heck, must be break time. I walked over to the water trough, washed away what little sweat I had managed to work up, and walked the short distance to the tracks. As I approached the crossing something looked very different but I didn't think about it enough to notice what it was. Finally, when I was only about a hundred feet from the rail it hit me: all the underbrush and growth along the right of way were gone, cleaned up, and the rails looked like a modern, working railroad, ready for train traffic. I had come by here on my way home from work the day before and it was as always, rusty rails and trees and shrubs, but now, here it was, all cleaned up and looking good.

As I stood on the road, between the rails, I thought I heard an old train whistle. I stood still, not breathing, listening and sure enough, there it was again, the sound of the old-time steam train whistles. I had heard them as a kid on the railroad that ran about a half mile from the farm on which I grew up. The whistle blew several more times as I stood listening, getting louder every time and I knew, somehow, there was a train coming down these old tracks, on this old abandoned line. I stepped back off the tracks and continued to listen and watch and soon I heard the unmistakable sound of the wheels clicking as they crossed the joints where the rails are bolted together, the old "clickety-clack" you always hear spoken of. The new modern trains don't sound like that any longer as they now have the quarter mile long rails, welded together to form a seamless, quiet ride. May have made a smoother ride, but it took away a sound that has been missed by me, and probably many others today. As I looked off to the left I could now see an oncoming headlight from the engine and I stood, mesmerized, unbelieving, listening to the whistle, the wheels, and watching the approaching headlight. Within a few minutes the most beautiful old "4-6-4 wheel" steam engine pulled up and stopped in front of me on the line. Every steam engine I had ever seen was black with colored trimmings. This one was beautiful, sparkling, shining white and the trim was gold. I don't know about metals like that but somehow I knew it was solid gold trimmings, not just paint. It had "No. 7" painted on the engine. As I started to walk along the engine, looking and marveling, I noticed the engineer in his compartment and said "good morning Sir" and he waved back. As I continued walking, now past the coal-tender, I thought how strange it was that the young engineer was wearing a perfectly, clean, white robe. He looked like what I thought an angel would look like. I noticed as I walked that there was not a smudge or a bit of dirt anywhere on the train. There were no bugs on the windshield or markings on the side where brush had rubbed it or anything. It was perfectly clean and unmarked. As I approached the passenger car, the conductor stepped down and stood beside the entrance. Again, another young man in a perfect, shining, white robe. I bid him a good morning, he responded, wishing me a good morning. I asked him if I could climb aboard and look the train over. "No Sir, I'm sorry, I can't allow that. The only ones who may board this train have a personal ticket from the King, without which you cannot enter. Although I see your name on a future manifest, you are not on this trip manifest, and I cannot let you on. Once on board this train nobody can exit until we reach our destination." "If I may Sir, what is your destination?" I asked. He responded, "Sir, you saw the number seven on the engine and you can see the name of the train on the side of the passenger car here, we are bound for glory, the next stop for this train is Heaven." As I looked through the windows of the passenger car I wondered at the youth and beauty of all the people onboard. All were smiling and happy. He stepped back on the car and I continued my walk around the rest of the train. As I passed the passenger car I noticed the name of the train, as the conductor had mentioned, and it all came to me then, making perfect sense. The train was called "The King's Express!" It was "No. 7," the number of perfection, the number of God. It was perfectly clean and shiny and white, as everything in glory would be. The engineer and conductor were indeed angels. The people onboard all looked young and beautiful, as we will when we get to Heaven and get our new bodies and new lives. "The King's Express" and it took a ticket from God himself to board this train. This was God's train, going back to Heaven and taking the souls of his saints' home. I stepped back a few more feet from the train and continued my walk around, but now felt like Moses at the burning bush. This was "hallowed" ground; I was intruding and wondered why I had been allowed to see this.

As I neared the engine on my walk back up the other side of the train I noticed out of the corner of my eye some movement on the road. I looked and it was Lucas and Miss Kate. They lived about a half a mile south of the tracks, we were a couple of hundred yards to the north, and they were our closest neighbors. Their kids were quite a few years older than ours but our two families had been very close. His daughters had been the baby-sitters for our children when we had to have one. We had seen them through the tough times with their kids and they with us through ours. We had spent many evenings together at each other's houses, knew each other's secrets and dreams and had become almost one family. During the winter I would often stop to check on them, see if they needed anything since I was going to town, keep them from having to go out, things like that, and during the summer we would often stop and pick them up and take them to the Dairy Queen with us. They were God-fearing folk and had raised great children. They were the kind of family we all hope to have. They were much more than friends. Many times if he was working on a Saturday, putting up hay in the summer, needing someone to haul in loads during harvest, things like this, Lucas would ask me if I would help him, since he knew I came from a farm and might enjoy getting back to the dirt. It was always my pleasure but Lucas never let me work for just the memory. At the end of the day he would thank me and then pull out his old wallet and pay me. He often used a phrase I heard my own father say when paying someone for helping him: "until you're better paid, thanks a lot." It was always a pleasure just being with them, excellent folks, great neighbors and the best of friends.

Lucas had been sick lately and when he walked anywhere Miss Kate had to help him and hold him up, but as they walked towards the train it seemed there was a spring in Lucas' step and Miss Kate was leaning on him, rather than the other way around as it had been lately. By now I was standing in front of the engine, on the road, and when they got to me, Lucas gave me a warm hand shake and said, "thanks for coming, I knew you would be here. When I knew I had this ride with destiny today I asked God if He would send someone kind, honest and decent to be with Miss Kate as I left, to walk her back home and be with her until the kids arrived to be with her. I'm glad he sent you. You were my choice but I couldn't suggest to my God, that wasn't my right." I followed in silence as they walked back towards the passenger car, where the conductor had gotten back down and was standing by the steps, waiting on his passenger. When they got to the steps, Lucas turned and took Miss Kate into his arms. I tried to back away, to give them privacy, but I felt this was as much for me to hear as for Lucas to say and for Miss Kate to understand, so I stood and listened, the conductor standing beside me, listening, his head bowed slightly, in respect to his passenger's final words to his partner of many, many years. "I have loved you Miss Katie, as much as was possible, for as long as I have known you. There were probably many times I let you down. There were many times I was ashamed I couldn't do more for you than I did, but you always seemed to understand and you never complained. You were my best friend, my partner, and an excellent mother to our children and a beautiful wife to me. I wish you could go with me now, just so you wouldn't have to be alone, but that is not my call, and you won't be alone. Even a few days from now, when this is all over and the kids go back to their respective homes, I will still be there with you, as will God, always. When you get back home, you will find a small gift that will stay with you forever. If you get lonely and miss me, just look at that gift and you will remember me, and it will make you smile. I must go now, there is a schedule to keep, but remember, I love you and will wait for you." With that Lucas turned and climbed the steps, the conductor right behind him, and the train started to roll. Through the window we saw a handsome, strong young man walk back to his seat and Miss Katie said, "look, there is Lucas. That is how he looked when he was young, before time took over as it does to all of us." We stood quietly and watched till the train was out of sight. We walked, without speaking, Miss Katie's arm through mine, all the way down to their farm. I could only imagine what was going on in Miss Katie's mind, as I knew what was going on in mine. God had let me see something so special because of the love of one of his saints.

When we got to their front door, on the table by the porch swing sat a beautiful crystal vase with the most perfect red roses I had ever seen.

The roses looked like they came from Heaven's own garden. This was the gift Lucas had told Miss Katie would be there for her. She bid me farewell, said she would be fine but wanted to call the kids and tell them of their father and I should go home. I walked back towards my place, still filled with wonder and awe and when I got to the crossing, it was all grown over and rusty again, as it always had been except for that short time about a half an hour before. I walked towards the creek to sit on the stump and think a bit. When I got there, there was an envelope and Lucas' old pocket watch, sitting on the stump, waiting for me. I opened the letter and read: "Thank-you my friend. I didn't want Miss Kate to be alone when I left. Thanks for walking her home. You used to enjoy this old watch so I thought maybe it should be with you as a reminder if you wouldn't mind keeping it for me. You were a good friend and a good neighbor, and so, until you are better paid, thanks a lot. Your friend in Christ, Lucas." This was an old watch, hadn't worked for years that used to sit on the coffee table at their house. Lucas had gotten it in Italy during WWII and even though it hadn't worked he kept if for the sentimental reasons it provided. As I sat there on the stump, the letter in my left hand, the old watch in my right hand, and tears streaming down my face, I felt my right hand getting warm. I opened my hand and looked and the second hand started moving and the watch started ticking, set at the correct time.

I stopped to see Miss Katie several times over the next few months, and still do on a regular basis and we sit and visit, about that day, about Lucas, and about the vase of roses, still beautiful, sitting on her kitchen table. She laughed one day and told me that those were still the original roses; she had never even so much as watered them. Said she knew they were special and that if she did anything to them at all it would be the wrong thing so she just enjoyed them as Lucas had told her. I told her I knew that and I told her the story of Lucas' old watch, which I had found on the stump after I had walked her home. She wasn't a bit surprised it was working and keeping perfect time, seemed to have expected it. She told me her kids accuse her of replacing the roses as they die, and she didn't even try to tell them the truth, knew they wouldn't believe it. All God-fearing born-again Christian children but she knew that would be more than they could understand. She and I are the only ones who know the truth and that is the way it will remain.

Her roses are still beautiful and always will be, and my old pocket watch sits on my desk, on top of my father's old Bible, still ticking and keeping perfect time. I have never wound it, doesn't need it, both it and the roses have been charged in Heaven.

THE REUNION

I went to the wall today, finally, after all these years. I went; I would like to say I went for the names I knew I would recognize, but that's not completely true. I would like to say I went for the countless other thousands whose names also appear on "the wall," but that's not completely true either. I also went for me. After all these years I went to see the man whose reflection looked back at me through the mirror finish of the wall, and find my way to his heart, if it was there. Those were tough times for us, as a country, and led to tough times for us as individuals, it became easy to become hard, build a shell around anything you had that faintly resembled soft, caring feelings. We became a culture of "who cares, it won't bother me" and as a country, and as individuals; we are just now coming out of it.

Nobody went to Vietnam to die, to get their name on a wall, a monument to those who stood and were counted, at a time when only the brave dared, because only the brave could stand tall and look the rest of the world in the eye, when our own country didn't know how to treat the heroes of the war that nobody wanted, so they were treated with indifference and often resentment, as though they were responsible for what they had the courage to face. We went in the service because it was our duty; they went to Vietnam because it was our generation's turn. They didn't start it, and weren't allowed to finish it, but by the thousands we went into the service, and by the thousands they went to Vietnam … we all went into the service with the cockiness of youth, and the feeling of living forever that God puts in all youth. These are the feelings that make our youth the prime of our life. We went in planning to live forever, and thousands came home in a flag draped box, to heartbroken parents, sobbing wives and lovers, tearful brothers and sisters, saddened friends and neighbors, and confused children. Nobody went in to die; their name on "the wall" was nobody's idea of immortality, but "duty, honor, and country" are still a very valued creed. Now all these years, the war long since ended, and all these years after the monument was erected, and dedicated to those "who paid the supreme sacrifice," I went to the wall ….

I went to the wall today, to talk, to listen, to visit the men, and to cry. The men were there also. I arrived late in the afternoon, nobody there but the ghosts, and me. Beautiful, calm, still evening, no breeze to move the bushes and leaves, so the rustling I heard as I stood and talked to them was them, standing behind me, shuffling their feet as they watched and moved, listening to me. As I talked they whispered in agreement and understanding, and every so often as the sun shone through a different tree, reflecting on "the wall," changing the shadows, I would see the reflection of a few of them, standing behind me. As I turned around to see them face-to-face they would fade back into my memory. My eyes were clouded over, hard to see, couldn't make out very many details, hard to see them very clear, but they were there. They knew why I had come, and they were there again for me, when I needed them, just as they were there years ago when we all needed them, and they were there. I went to apologize to the heroes I knew, and to thank the others. I was too many years in coming; I owed my friends more respect than to show up years late. I owed the other heroes more respect than to show up years late, but they understood. Odd isn't it? Years ago they understood and went, and now, once again, it is them that understand when it takes me years to come see them, the heroes in death even as they were heroes in life. Why was it always them that had to understand?

I went to the wall today, and cried. Tears from the soul, that after all these years, started to melt the hard shell that was built by so many, years ago, and only now starting to soften. Several of them standing behind me understood the tears and even shed a few with me. Only they would understand the meaning of the small gift I laid at their feet, only they understand the meaning of all the gifts that have been brought to them through the years. Times change, the country has changed, homage is being paid, heroes are being honored, and shells are beginning to fall away. Time changes all things, even nations and hard hearts. It's been over twenty years, since then I have heard little children laugh and giggle, I have watched young lovers walk hand in hand in the rain, I have held soft warm women, and felt their warmth, clear down to the shell. I have watched my own children grow, from innocent helpless babies, to young adults, and have known the pride of parenthood. I have watched elderly people walking slowly down the sidewalk, leaning on each other, drawing strength from the other when theirs isn't enough to make it on their own. I have watched loved ones pass away, and realized it is okay to feel loss, and that no life lived was a loss, and no loss goes unnoticed or unfelt by others. I have known love, laughter, sadness, warmth, caring, and as I stood at the wall, crying for lost love and innocence, I understood..

We all did what we had to do at the time, and we all have to live with the consequences of our actions. Nobody will ever have to explain the actions of others, just of themselves. I am sorry for the years lost, not facing myself and those I should have visited years ago. When I realized that they understood my feelings, I finally understood myself. If we all had to do again what we did years ago, most of us would do it all the same way, and as I listened to them talk, other than the pain their passing did to their loved ones back home, they would make the same sacrifice again, for "duty, honor and country" is a creed that only the strongest of heroes are capable of living up to, and only the strongest and bravest are named, by the thousands, name after name after name. Time had gotten away from me, shadows were too long, darkness falling, and still my eyes were too cloudy to read the names of those I knew, so I didn't look for the individual names, but rather saluted them all, said my good-bye and walked away, but as I left, even though a small breeze had started, I heard them all tell me good-bye, they'll see me the next time. It was them talking, not the leaves rustling, as they walked with me to my car, and walked back again as I sat there waiting for my eyes to clear.

I went to the wall today, and left with a much more peaceful feeling than I had arrived with. As I sat there and thought of us, years ago, the thought flashed through my mind of my own children, and their generation, and their turn. After a split-second thought of my children and their safety, I smiled, confident that when it was their turn, they would stand and be counted, as every generation before them has. My only fear was that of a parent. Could I live with their cockiness and thoughts of immortality? Could I live with the thought of losing them as every generation of parent has worried since time began, of losing their children? As in the past, every generation had it's turn to rule the universe, and when their time comes, I will let them go, just as our parents let us go, some to return as we did, and some to return as those on "the wall" had; in flag draped boxes, to heartbroken parents, sobbing wives and lovers ... "duty, honor and country" ... only the brave can stand that tall and be counted. Nobody went to die, but in his or her own way all achieved his or her immortality, as we all thought we would. GOD BLESS AMERICA, and thank-you for a country worth dying for, and that their deaths were not in vain, no life lived to the fullest is ever a loss. I went to the wall today, and I cried, for lost love, lost youth, lost innocence, lost life, lost time, hardened hearts, second chances, lost laughter, lost friends, and the chance to have found them all again. I went to the wall today… I'll go again, I owe them…

THE TEARS OF GOD

On Thursday evening Jesus had supper with his disciples in what was to become known as the "upper room." They ate what was to become known as the "last supper." It was here that Jesus introduced them to what would become known as the "Holy Communion" or "The Lord's Supper." He broke the bread and said, "Take, eat, this is my body that is given for you. This do in remembrance of me." The same with the wine, he said, "This is my blood in the new testament which is shed for you." It was here that he also announced that he was going to be betrayed and that it was Judas who was to betray him. After they left the upper room, they went to the Mount of Olives, where Peter expressed his love and faithfulness to Jesus, only to be told that before the rooster would crow, he would deny Jesus three times. Then Jesus took Peter and the sons of Zebedee, James and John, and went to the Garden of Gethsemane. While in the garden, Jesus prayed three times, earnestly, pleading, so hard that he sweat drops of blood, asking "if there be any other way Father, remove this cup from me, but, nevertheless, not my will but thy will be done." Then a crowd of soldiers and temple guards approached Jesus to take Him prisoner. Peter drew his sword and cut off one of the ears of one of the servants of the High Priest. Jesus told Peter to put away his sword, saying,

"The cup which my Father has given me, shall I not drink it?" Jesus was then taken into custody, to be taken for His trial, and all of his followers deserted him and ran away. Jesus was put on trial where there were no honest charges against him, only lies and stories. He was nevertheless beaten, whipped, a crown of thorns pushed down on his head, ridiculed and mocked. Sentenced to death by a human court. The following morning, Friday, at about the third hour, or at nine in the morning, Jesus was nailed to the cross. Jesus hung on the cross for roughly six hours, during the course of which at one point he cried out, "My God, my God, why hast thou forsaken me?" What was the cup Jesus asked to have removed from him and why had God forsaken His own son?

Before creation, before even the angels had been created, God was. God always was, ever since the beginning, before there was any time to record, before there was even time. God the Father, God the Son, and God the Holy Spirit; three in one, always, together, in perfect harmony and unison. Always one thought pattern, always the same, never a disagreement, never any conflict, only perfect harmony and unison. What one thought was what was thought by the others, always. God is, and always was, One, and yet three. The perfect mind of God was always exactly the same. In the first chapter of the Bible, Genesis chapter 1, verse 26, God said, "Let us make man in our image." Let us, not I will, not we should, not an individual, but more than one: Us! From the beginning God the Father, God the Son, and God the Holy Spirit were one, they were God! At no time since the beginning had they ever been separated in any way or fashion, never apart, always One. Perfect harmony, perfect peace, and perfectly aligned in every way, always together, always pure and perfect.

Every word I have written thus far is true and from God's Word, the Bible. I have added nothing to these words, and I will add nothing to the Word of God. In the last chapter of the Bible, Revelations chapter 22, verse 18, it says, "If any man shall add unto these things, God shall add unto him the plagues that are written in this book." I believe every word God has said and written in the Bible and I fear Him who can destroy not only my body, but also my eternal soul, and I will not add to the words of God. I am not a learned man but as a human, God has given me the free will and imagination that we all have. I have read many writings and heard many speeches and sermons from learned men, and I have read these writings in the Bible, I have spent time in prayer over these things, and I also have my thoughts on what is meant in places where there is no clear explanation of some things.

What was the cup that Jesus asked to have removed from Him, and why did God forsake Him as he hung on the cross? Was Jesus afraid to die? Most emphatically, No! In the first place, Jesus said that no man could take His life; He had the power to lay down His life and to take it up again. At His trial Jesus was sentenced to death. Who do we humans think we are that we can sentence God to death anyway? Ever since the beginning Jesus knew He would come into this world to die. This is why He was born into this world; that He might die to save mankind from their sins. No, Jesus was not afraid to die; He willingly came into this world to do exactly that. I honestly believe that Jesus looked forward to fulfilling the will and desire of the Father. Was Jesus afraid of Satan? Absolutely not! Since when is the Creator afraid of the created? The only power the devil has is that which Jesus has given him. Satan is referred to as the "Prince of this world." Jesus is the "King of this world," and in no time, and in no place in history has the prince ever held power over the King. No power can stand against the Lord and Satan is no exception. No, I assure you, Jesus held no fear of the devil. Was Jesus afraid of failure? I'm sorry, is this not He who created the world? I love Genesis chapter 1. God spoke and the heavens, the earth, all the animals, all the birds, all the fishes, everything was created and came into being. From nothing came everything. The sun was hung in space as a light and it has never burned out, never moved, never a problem. The planets are where they are by the word of God. Everything is perfect by the spoken word of God. Six times in the first book of the Bible a verse ends with the words "and God saw that it was good." The sixth time it even says that it was "very good." After every day's creation God saw that it was good. No redo, no corrections, nothing to adjust, perfection, pure and simple. No, Jesus was not afraid of failure. Was Jesus afraid of disappointing the Father? God is pure, perfect and true. He has never changed His mind and decided to give up on something He had done. When Jesus was baptized and emerged, the Father said, "This is my beloved Son in whom I am well pleased." No, Jesus was not afraid The Father would change His mind and be ashamed of Him. God is always true and faithful, that is one thing we can count on. Was Jesus afraid of sin? Since the beginning God knew that sin would enter this world and at the same time Jesus knew he would come into this world to save the world from it's sin. Jesus was born a human man. God himself visited the earth and Jesus; the Son of God became the son of man. Jesus is the only perfect man who ever lived on this earth. The perfect God became the perfect man. While on this earth Jesus walked with sinners, talked with sinners, ate with sinners, healed sinners and announced that He came to save the sinners. Sin held no fear for Jesus. Even when tempted by Satan himself He had no fear for he knew The Father was with him. No, Jesus had no fear of sin.

What then was this cup? I believe the cup Jesus asked to have removed was the separation that would come from The Father once Jesus had taken my sins onto him. God being perfect, and since He was also God, Jesus himself being perfect, and although God loves sinners, He can have no part of sin; none whatsoever, no part. God hates sin, despises it. God loves the sinners but has always hated sin, and this was no different. Even though it was His own Son, and even though Jesus had committed no sin, He became sin when He took my sin onto Him, and The Father, in his perfect, pure way had to distance himself from His own son. This would have been almost more than He could bear. Ever since the beginning, eons ago, Jesus had been One with The Father, always, perfect, and the thought of not being one with His Father was almost overwhelming to Him. Once He took my sin onto him, becoming sin for me, going to my cross, dying my death, He was alone. Alone, with all of my sins on Him, all of the sins of the entire world on Him, alone, being forsaken by His own Father. Jesus was not afraid of dying, sin, failure, the devil, nothing, no fear, and at being forsaken he wasn't afraid, just completely overwhelmed and heart-broken. "My God, my God, why hast thou forsaken me?" Forgive me Jesus, for it was because of me that you were forsaken. The Father didn't stop loving you, not at all, He loved you so much, you were doing the will of The Father, but because of me you were alone on the cross, forsaken by The Father; the most high, holy, pure, perfect Father. Jesus knew He was doing the will of The Father, and knew that they would become one again, but for this brief time He was separated. At the end of His life, after all the prophecies had been fulfilled, Jesus said "It is finished." Another account says that Jesus said, "Father into thy hands I commit my spirit." Jesus knew He was doing the will of The Father and knew that His Father loved Him, and knew that they would be one again, but it must have been a terrible feeling for that perfect body to have the weight of my sin thrust upon it, and at the same time have The Father forsake him, too much for even Jesus to bear almost.

The Bible says that God saves the tears of the saints. It records that Jesus wept at the grave of his dear friend Lazarus. He also wept as he beheld Jerusalem, knowing what would happen there in a few short years when the temple would be destroyed. At no place that I can find does it ever record that The Father wept. Again, I am not adding to the Word of God, but I have to wonder if The Father didn't weep when He beheld His son. When my son was very young he faced surgery and I cried for him. My love for my son is nothing compared to the love The Father has for his children, and Jesus was His only begotten Son. The rest of us are sons and daughters of God by adoption, but Jesus was the only begotten Son of The Father. I imagine it being very quiet in Heaven from Thursday evening until Friday evening, as The Father witnessed the abuse and cruelty dealt to His son, and then witnessed His son hanging on the cross. A cross belonging to me, dying for sins that didn't belong to Him, but rather to me, and hearing His son cry out to him in anguish, "… why hast thou forsaken me?" I can imagine Jesus being surrounded by millions of angels, most with their swords drawn, awaiting the word to rescue their Lord, witnessing Him being beaten, whipped, watching the crown of thorns being pounded down onto his brow. They watched Him being nailed to my cross. I can imagine another million or so angels surrounding the throne of The Father, the Great White Throne, begging permission to go save their Lord, their Jesus, He who they had known forever since their creation, and He who they had watched grow-up as a little boy when He had been born a human, the son of man. God assigns angels to watch over each and every one of us, every child born has angels, and many of these had maybe been assigned to watch over Jesus as a small boy as he grew into manhood, and now they watched as He was treated like this. I imagine they begged God to let them intervene, and I can imagine God watching His Son, and looking at each of the angels and then saying, "No my sons, sheath your swords, this must happen, for this reason He came into this world and for this purpose He must die on the cross." But… this was God's Son, and I can imagine the quiet and silence as tears rolled down the magnificent face of the Most High God as he watched His perfect Son, alone, suffer and die on the cross in my place. I have to ask, Father in Heaven, who caught your tears as you watched your son die so that I might live? Whenever I am hurt or heart-broken you hold me and catch my tears. You are the ultimate authority, there is none above you, who held you and caught your tears as your son died in my place? ....And through all this, God still loves me. He always has and He always will. He doesn't love me less when I disobey and He doesn't love me more when I obey, He loves me with the perfect love that only God can.

... my Jesus I love thee, I know thou art mine..... For thee all the pleasures of sin I resign....

To The Victor

In 1832 New York Senator William Marcy coined a phrase that has been used and over-used to the point of having lost some of its flavor. "To the victor go the spoils." Winner takes all, he who wins the war wins all that was fought for; you not only lose the war, you lose your land, your women, your possessions, all you had; to the victor go the spoils. Way back before that, in the days of the Roman Army and the days of Rome's supremacy, it was much different. The armies did the fighting, the dirty work, and the generals reaped the harvest, getting all they wanted from the defeated army or country. Also during the days of the Roman rule, there were gladiators and other fighting men who fought for a much higher prize: their lives. If they were victorious in their battle of the day, they lived to fight another day. To lose meant to die, and I believe life took on a much higher meaning for those who fought only to live. There was no glory, there were no slaves to take, there was no gold to hoard, no money to count, nothing other than their life. If they won the day's battle, they lived to sup, sleep, and awaken to another day of the same, but for them life had meaning. To them the air smelled sweeter, the meal was more refreshing, even though not a delicacy, the sunset was more beautiful and the sunrise the next day held more promise. There was living attached to each breath they had, each thought they entertained, and to each day they survived. The life they lived was real; it was something to be lived, loved and enjoyed, day by day. Without even knowing it, they lived Matthew 6:34 to the limit: "so don't worry about tomorrow, for tomorrow will bring its own worries." They lived for today, enjoyed today, and they let tomorrow take care of itself; and I believe the lives they lived were lives lived to the fullest.

I recently visited with a dear friend of mine, one who was in the midst of, or in the finishing stages of, taking the cure for a diagnosis of breast cancer. It was good to see her and I tried very hard to convey the happiness I felt for her, but was meeting much resistance. I finally asked her how it felt to be a "winner" in such a tough, ugly, fight for her very life. "Winner," she asked? "In what way do you figure I am a winner? I can't stand to look at myself in the mirror, my eyes are sunken, surrounded by black circles, I have lost my hair, after surgery I am missing a part of my body, a part that is supposed to make a difference in the way a woman is perceived, I find myself unattractive and have no idea why a man would find me any different, my body ravaged by the disease, the cure, and the surgery, I have a tube in my body that drains any and all infections, draining a vile, disgusting liquid, I had a tube in me that was used to administer the chemo, a poison poured into my body to kill an even uglier poison, I can't stand the smell of most foods that I once loved, can't taste most foods, find salty foods sweet and find sweet foods that I once loved to taste salty and unsavory, have no stamina, easily tired, can fall asleep and take a nap after only being awake for an hour or so, anything and everything that I have ever known myself to be is now gone or changed, I am a completely different person than I was a mere four to six months ago, and I don't like who or what I have become and you ask me how it feels to be a winner? I am sorry I don't share your enthusiasm or your excitement at my current lot in life. I am glad I am alive, but I have no idea for how long, nor do I know what the remainder of my life will amount to, and you call me a winner? I thank-you very much for your faith in me and your kind words, but you need to do some talking to convince me of what you are talking about."

I apologized sincerely, hoping I had not offended her too deeply, for I have never been in her shoes, I have never been diagnosed with cancer, and I have never fought the fight she fought, and still fights on a daily basis, and will continue to fight for the rest of her life, but I continued on with my thoughts and comments. "My next comment may offend you, and I hope it does not, but it will not make sense to you, but I feel the need to say it anyway: In a way, in your suffering, in my ignorance, in my lack of empathy for I have never been where you are, and I have never walked where you walk, I envy you the closeness you have acquired with Jesus through all your trials. I awaken in the morning, start my coffee, read my Bible, meet with my Lord, and say my prayers, and I know that my prayers are heard and that I am speaking with my Lord and Savior, and I know that I am in a special place, for prayer with the Lord is a very special place, but you; for you it is different. You awaken in the morning, start your coffee if the smell of it doesn't make you sick now, if you are still able to drink it, you read your Bible, and you meet with your Lord, but in a much different way. Jesus smiles at me when we meet, and he accepts me as I am. When you meet with Jesus, there is a fire in your eyes and the same fire in His eyes as you gaze upon Him the first time in the morning. For you it is different. You have walked through the 'valley of the shadow' with Him, and He lead you every step of the way, never once leaving you alone. He took you to the ring where you entered and fought with death, and Jesus was your corner-man. You fought till you could fight no more, and then Jesus gave you His strength to continue the fight. When you were too tired to stand any longer, He let you lean on Him, and when it had gone on long enough, death backed into his corner and conceded the round. You won the round, not on your own, for without Jesus you wouldn't even have made it into the ring, but you won the round. No, you will not win the fight, none of us ever do and you won't either. You may never lose to death because of the cancer, it may come after you again in a month or a year or even ten years, or maybe never, and you may pass peaceably in your sleep in thirty years from any number of things, but ultimately, eventually, death will win, he always does, but, until that final heartbeat, you have won. You are a winner and you have earned the right to wear the pink ribbon that so many wear to show their support for you and those like you who have won. Eventually we all lose, but until that day, you have won, and you are a winner, and there is closeness between you and Jesus that those of us who have never walked the valley of the shadow can know or understand. On that day when we all stand before the Lord, brand new and perfect, in our Heavenly, glorious bodies, I believe you and those like you will be in the front of the crowd, ready to enter Paradise, for your new body will no longer bear the scars of the battle; that ugly battle which you won, with the help of the Lord Jesus beside you, carrying you when you just had nothing left, but He would not let you quit and you didn't have it in you to quit anyway."

Yes, you won. The black circles will fade away from around your eyes, your cheeks will fill out again, your hair will grow back, and you will learn to mask the missing part of your body, and you are and always will be special and attractive for what you think you are missing, you are actually gaining, because you fought the fight, not alone, but with the Lord, and He doesn't lose and never will. Yes, you won, and I envy you the closeness with which you walk with the Lord during the days now. It is a special place beside Him, with looks between the two of you that are understood only by the two of you. It is a place you have earned, a spot you have the right to walk. God has never lost before and He will not start now and yes, you are a winner. Wear the pink ribbon proudly, it is the only way we mere mortals can tell we are walking with a soldier of the Lord, who has walked through the valley of the shadow of death, accompanied by the Lord, and the rest of it is all personal and private between the two of you. You have the love and respect of the rest of us, and yes, Jesus knows what you have been through, you didn't go through it alone, He was always with you and He knows what it felt like. During those long, cold, lonely nights when you cried and asked God where He was and why He was allowing this and you questioned Him, He not only understood your questions, but He wept with you. As Jesus stood at the grave of Lazarus, He was so touched by the sadness of Lazarus' sisters that He stood and wept, knowing that in just mere moments He would raise Lazarus from the dead. Yes, Jesus knew of your sadness and He felt it with you, and yes, He wept with you. You were never alone in your struggle. I like the gladiators, the winner got life, life abundant, and worth the living. You won, and you live to fight and hopefully win another day. To you life is very special. The air tastes sweeter and the sun rises so much more beautiful, and even in a storm you find the calm. You won my gladiator friend, congratulations; you and the Lord are one and have won, even if only until the next battle, but yes, you won.

Be strong and of a good courage, fear not, nor be afraid of them: for the Lord thy God, he it is that doth go with thee; he will not fail thee, nor forsake thee. Deuteronomy 31:6

Too Late

Jacob liked his Saturday mornings. This was the end of a good week. His in-laws had been here since Sunday afternoon, spent a few days, had a good time, and then Wednesday morning they had left, taking his wife Angie and his two daughters home with them for a few days. It was only a two hour drive and he would leave about noon today and go spend a few days with them and then on Tuesday afternoon they would all come back home. His life was good, all the way around and he was very happy with it. He would pick up the mail as he came in the house in the evening, sort it, put the bills and anything else he was interested in reading on his desk, in neat piles, then on Saturday morning he would sleep in, get up around six or so, make some coffee and come into his office. Turn on the radio, read the mail, pay the bills and relax, here in the comfort of his "home" office. He was only 36 years old and already the President of the largest bank in town. Aggressive, smart, terribly arrogant, thought quite a bit of himself but who knows, maybe he thought he had that right. He had done well for himself in such a short time.

As he came in the house last evening he had not even sorted the mail. With his wife gone and he going to be gone for a few days next week he had stayed late at work the past few evenings getting things caught up. Came in the house last evening, put all the mail on his desk and sat down to relax. As he listened to the music, drinking his coffee, he sorted through yesterday's mail. Here was another envelope from his dad, found it stuck in the mailbox along with the mail. He knew it was from his dad, always read the same way, "to my son Jacob." Hadn't seen his folks for almost 3 years now, last time had shamed him and embarrassed him and he still wasn't ready to be decent about it. He had received 2 birthday cards and 3 Christmas cards since then and hadn't opened a one of them. His dad had called but Jacob wouldn't answer, if his wife did he made her hang up on him, wouldn't return a call or anything. Like I said, pretty arrogant and regarded himself a bit too highly. As he held the envelope he remembered the last time he had seen his parents. It was his last promotion and a couple of friends from the bank and their wives had taken him and his wife out for supper. Nice restaurant and there, on the other side of the restaurant sat his dad and mom. Place was crowded so he didn't have to wave or anything like that, but as his folks got up to leave they spotted Jacob and Angie and came by the table to say hello. His mom bent down and kissed him on the cheek and his dad had patted his shoulder and they had both said hello. Jacob jumped up and told them he was busy and asked them not to bother him in public like that again. As his folks turned to leave one of the gentlemen at the table commented on how rude Jacob had been. His response was that "they are just my parents, not that important. Dad is just an old truck driver and Mom was just a cook at a little diner down the road. Not really much for parents. They seem to always have to come up and embarrass me in public. Did you see the old coat Mom was wearing and did you notice the frayed cuff on Dad's shirt?" Yeah, like I said, thought quite a bit of himself, not enough of his parents. There was something about the envelope he was still holding though. Not too sure why but for some reason he thought he would read it, after he was done with all the "important" mail and paying his bills.

Well, he paid the few bills he had received, read a couple of other pieces of mail, but his eyes and his thoughts kept returning to the envelope from his dad. Something bothered him about it, looked like some water had splattered on it and then dried. Finally he could not think of any more reasons to put it off and besides, this one bothered him. He had received another note from his dad on Wednesday, was in with the mail when he brought it in but he just threw it in the wastebasket by the desk, unopened. He opened the envelope, unfolded the letter which was also spotted with a few drops of water. He hadn't read but a few lines when he realized it wasn't water, they were the tears of his dad, and he added his own as he read:

"My son Jacob… I don't even know if you will read this, you don't seem to read the cards I send, nor do you answer the phone calls or listen to the messages I leave, but I had to try one more time to reach you. We buried your mom today. She passed away about the middle of the morning on Wednesday. I was outside and had just come in to check on her, make sure all was well, and found her in her easy chair. She was holding the stack of cards she had received from you through the years, and she had the picture of you and her at the carnival when you were about fifteen or so. She had just passed away as her cheeks were still wet with the tears she had shed in the last few minutes of her life. I held her and told her good-bye for a few minutes and then called the police and they arrived in a few minutes with the coroner and an ambulance. There was nothing they could do so they gently and quietly carried her out to the ambulance and took her to the hospital for an autopsy since she had died at home. I called your house several times and left messages but you never called back so I drove over and left a note in your mailbox but you never responded. I called the bank but they always tell me you are busy with a client. I realize you are just avoiding me and instruct your staff to get me off the phone. I know you were ashamed of us Jacob, I remember your comments in the restaurant a few years back, when you thought we couldn't hear you, but my golly son, this was your mom. This was the woman who gave you life, who took care of you when you were sick, cooked your favorite meals to make you happy, helped you with your homework, and loved you unconditionally. If you hate me or refuse to talk to me that is one thing, but she was your mom, all she ever did was love you and wish you the best of everything. I ordered a nice flower from your family for the visitation and the funeral so folks would think you cared. I believe most knew the truth and just didn't ask because they didn't want to hurt me even more than your absence already had. The service was nice; the preacher said a lot of nice things about her. It was at the church where you went to Sunday school and where you got married and where you went till you got a little too important for God. Your mom died still loving you Jacob and so do I still. I'm sorry for everything that you think was done wrong to you and against you. Sorry to bother you son but I thought you should know, even if you didn't want to. I love you, dad"

Jacob must have read the letter five or six times, crying harder each time. He ran to the phone where he had just reset the machine, rather than wiping the messages out and listened to each call from his dad on Wednesday. His heart broke as he heard his dad's voice crack and choke up on the message he tried to leave. He ran back to the waste basket by the desk and dug out the note from Wednesday night's mail and opened it and read: "my son Jacob, please call me as soon as you get this, I have some very sad news for you. Love you, dad." He ran to the stack of newspapers waiting for the recycle truck and got the paper for Thursday. He opened to the obituary section, which he never usually read; just life stories of old dead people, and read the obituary of his own mom. He sobbed audibly when he read the part about her being "survived by her loving husband and her loving son Jacob." The medical examiner had been able to find no reason for her death, it was deemed that she had died of a broken heart, and Jacob knew the reason for that. He opened the top drawer of the desk and pulled out the cards from his dad for his birthdays and Christmas and opened each one and read them then, as he should have done when he received them, sobbing as he felt his dad's love pouring through the simple words, all from the heart.

He sat there surrounded by cards, notes and memories… beautiful, soft, sweet memories, each one torturing his soul a little more than the others. After about an hour or two he finally cried himself out. He called his wife, told her what had happened, and then called the number he had known so well, all his life, and when the phone was answered he hardly recognized the voice, his dad had aged terribly in the past few days, barely recognizable as he said "hello," and paused, waiting for a response and after a few seconds said "hello" again, and this time Jacob managed to say between his sobs… "Hello Dad, it's me, Jacob… I am so sorry… please forgive me… "

Boast not thyself of to morrow; for thou knowest not what a day may bring forth. Proverbs 27:1

Uncle Andy

"**D**ad … Dad … wake up, wake up Dad … c'mon, wake up … " Uncle Andy heard the plea and knew it was for him but couldn't come out of the fog, he was halfway between asleep and awake, and he didn't recognize the voice. It was neither of his sons' nor his daughter's voice, but knew it was for him and couldn't figure who would be calling him "Dad." He fought himself awake and as he turned over in bed and saw the young face before him he knew right away; it was his son Wayne. Wayne had been born severely handicapped. He had never spoken, nor had he ever been able to move under his own power. He had been completely and wholly dependent upon others caring for his every need. I don't know how much he had been able to see or hear or to understand, but he was the third son of my Uncle Andy and Aunt Rosella, born in 1954, the younger brother of Max and Roy, and the older brother of Christine. He lived until his mid-teens, at which time he had gone home to be with his Heavenly Father.

"What are you doing here Wayne?" Andy asked as he rolled over and sat up on the edge of the bed. "I always wondered what you would have sounded like, what you would have looked like standing, walking, smiling, or just being here … this is great … what are you doing here ... why are you here ... is this real or a dream ... how long are you staying ... have you seen your mom yet ... what's going on ... talk to me ... tell me something ... I have a million questions for you." Wayne laughed and said, "Hold on Dad, I can explain everything but you need to calm down and let me talk for a few minutes. I can answer all your questions but you have to let me tell the story from the beginning, not just jump in and go from wherever." Andy got that big Bauer grin on his face and said, "Ok, go ahead, but first allow me one pleasure... I have always wanted to tell you that I loved you and knew you heard it and understood it and now, after all this time, I have my chance, so, Wayne, I love you... I always did and I always will." At that Wayne laughed and got that same grin on his face and said, "I know Dad, and I thank you for that, and I love you, and that is as good a place to start this story as any, so here goes ..."

"Often times from Heaven I have been allowed to look down on you and Mom and my family. The Heavenly Father knew what it was like for me on earth and that I never had a chance to know any of you, nor to enjoy the life that was here but unavailable to me. The Father has told me stories about you and Mom and what great parents you were, how you cared for me, how you loved me, how you doted on me, and how either of you would have traded your lives if I could have had a normal life as my brothers and sister did. He told me how you did all that could be done for me at the time and how at times, alone, in the dark, you had each wept for me. You never once wept out of sympathy for yourselves, but out of care and love for me." Wayne continued then with, "A while back, time in Heaven is much different than that on earth, I was watching as Mom was checking you into the home in Paxton. She fluffed your pillow, tucked you in, smiled at you, talked to you, told you how much she loved you, and did her best to act like this was just another day or so in a perfect life. I watched her spend the remainder of the day with you and I watched her as she went home that night. She walked into the house, into every room, looking at what would never be the same again, walked back out to the living room, sat in your chair, talked to you a while, to God a while, to herself a while, then got up, went into the bedroom, got ready for bed and got into bed on your side, where she has slept every night since. She was tired and dropped off to sleep quickly, but as she slept she wept. I tried to catch her tears but couldn't, and realized it didn't matter because God was catching them. He catches the tears of the saints, and He caught all of Mom's tears that night, and has every night since. Heaven is a happy place, no tears, no regrets, no sadness, but God knew something was wrong and asked me about it. We spoke of you and Mom and He asked if I would like to spend a day on earth with you since I didn't have the chance when I was alive. I asked if that would be possible and God smiled and said that of course it was possible, anything is possible. He sent me down this morning to spend your last day on earth with you, to do anything either of us want to do, go anywhere we want and have fun and enjoy each other's company … so, where do you want to go Dad, and what do you want to do?"

Andy grinned again and said it didn't matter; he just wanted to spend the day with Wayne, so he asked him where he wanted to go. Wayne said he just wanted to see where his dad had grown up, see the family, see what his dad did, see his dad's life before he, Wayne, had been born. Instantly they were on the farm out in Fountain Creek where Andy had grown up. He was just a young man, the family was there having a get-together and Wayne stood there amidst all of them, watching, listening, grinning and absolutely loving what he was finally experiencing. Andy stood there watching with tears in his eyes as his son finally walked, laughed, ran around, climbed up in the barn, ran on the same yard that Andy ran on. At one point Wayne came back to Andy and asked if "that man over there is my Uncle Ray?" Andy looked at where Wayne was pointing and said that yes that is his uncle. Wayne smiled and said he knew that and that he hadn't changed much, would have recognized him anywhere. Andy smiled as he realized that Ray had died years before Wayne had been born, during WWII and that Wayne knew him from seeing him in Heaven. After Wayne enjoyed all of the family for a while, they left there and were instantly at the marriage ceremony where Andy and Rosella were saying their wedding vows. Wayne watched this very soberly, amazed, interested and happy. They went to the place they lived over the Legion Home in Cissna Park, down by the fertilizer plant that Andy had owned, into the new house east of town, all over, to the high school gym to watch his kids play basketball and all sports, places that meant so much to Andy and now meant so much to Wayne, to finally get to see after all of this time. They spent the day together, laughing, and visiting and Andy enjoyed what he had dreamed of so often; time with his son Wayne, quality time with his son. Finally Wayne said they needed to go as it was getting late in the afternoon and they had to be back shortly. As they walked they talked and Andy told Wayne how much this had meant to him but that he felt bad, Wayne hadn't spent much time with his mother. Wayne said that was fine as God had told him that he would get to spend her last day with her also, but he grinned and looked at his dad and said that he enjoyed it when he had heard him refer to his mom as "Rosie." He said he thought that was a nice nickname and he enjoyed it.

As they entered Andy's room, he was just passing, and Wayne leaned over and kissed his mom on the cheek. Through her tears Rosella smiled, squeezed Andy's hand and said, "Good-bye my love, and thank-you. I just felt Wayne's presence in this room and figured God had sent him to take you back home. I'm glad you'll have him there to show you around. Tell him I love him too and I'll see you both soon." With that, Wayne on one side of Andy, and Jesus on the other side, they slipped the bonds of this earth and entered Heaven's glory, to be there forever.

On Tuesday, 25 September 2012, the day that would have been his 91st birthday, as Andy would look down to make sure his love of over 60 years was okay, he would see the military graveside rites being administered as his earthly body was being returned to the earth from where it had come. He would have been pleased I believe. You have been well blessed Uncle Andy, welcome home! You are now, and always will be one of God's soldiers, and we will miss you here on earth.

When I Was Hungry

"It's rough out there Tookie, looks like we have a car in trouble about a half mile north of us here, guess I need to go see whether I can help them." Bob had just come in from a nasty, cold, raging blizzard which had been hammering them for the better part of the day and here it was now, coming onto nightfall. His wife's name was Martha but he had called her "Tookie" ever since they had married, right after he had returned from Vietnam in the late '60s. He had been sent to a school in Houston for six weeks training before being deployed and there was a little place on the coast, east of Houston, called Tookie's where he had gone every Saturday evening for a cheeseburger and a beer or two as he thought of his home, family and all his friends, as every member of the service probably always has and probably always will. There is always a place inside you that is homesick while you are in the service, even when surrounded by all your new friends and those you are being trained to trust with your life as you are being trained to protect their life. He did his tour, was wounded twice, awarded two purple hearts and the bronze star for bravery and after his discharge came home to marry and return to the farming life he had loved for as long as he could remember. One of the soft memories he had of that part of his life was the time he had spent at Tookie's and that became the pet name for his wife. He was unable to get any land for his own so he took a job with a big farmer he had known all his life and spent the next 40 years as a hired hand on a large grain and cattle farm. Three years ago the farmer he had worked for his entire life had passed away leaving the farm to his son. The boy was a good farmer but didn't have the heart his father had and after another six months or so had told Bob that he was getting too old to do the job any longer and had let him go to be replaced by a younger man. Bob and Martha had been told they could continue to live on the farmstead where they had lived since their marriage, where they had raised their kids, and the only home they or their family had ever known. It had been a good life, but things changed now. Being a hired hand never paid all that well but Bob had the use of the pick-up truck for the farm, a big garden at the edge of the field behind the house, they had been given a hog and half of a beef every year at butcher time, so even though they didn't have much money, they had what they had needed. Since he had been let go all of those benefits other than the garden had gone away. Now they had the house and the Social Security they had qualified for, but that wasn't much either as their pay had never been that much while working. Things were just plain tough but they did the best they could, and they managed to get by without a lot of the things they called luxuries that most people just called basics.

The farmer still kept a lot of equipment in the shed on the farm there and Bob had been given permission to use any of the tractors or whatever he needed for moving snow or anything else he would need. It was getting dark enough outside now that as they looked out of the kitchen window they could see the headlights of the car about a half mile north of the house and the headlights were pointing off at an angle into the field. It was obvious they were stuck in a drift or had maybe even slid off the road into the ditch. It was just plain inhuman to even consider not helping them. They had no idea who was in the car but knew that was no place to spend the night or the duration of the blizzard until a plow could make it down the road, and if they ran out of gas they weren't going to live through the night. It was just plain cold, down close to zero with a miserable wind-chill. They both knew what they had to do and as Bob put on his heavy clothes he laughed and commented to Martha that this was not how he had planned to spend Christmas Eve.

Finally, dressed as warm as he could get, Bob went out and started the tractor with the scoop on the front and the blade on the back. Thought he would need them definitely. As the tractor motor warmed-up Bob put a couple of chains and a shovel on the tractor in case he needed to scoop snow to get under the car to hook a chain. Finally, ready, he opened the door, backed the tractor out and drove past the house on the way to the road. As he drove past the house he saw Martha standing at the window and waved to her. She waved back and he could see the worry in her face. She was a good woman and he thought of her as he plowed through the snow towards the car. When he was about fifty feet away he saw the car had ridden up on the top of a drift and it had thrown it towards the ditch, and it was definitely stuck, not going anywhere on its own power. He continued to scoop and move snow until he had reached the front of the car. He walked to the passenger side of the car and they rolled the window down. He saw a man, woman and three small children, all probably less than ten years old. He told them he would hook a chain to the front of the car and pull them free from the snow, then stop and unhook the chain and they could follow him to his place. He would plow a path for the car and when they arrived at the farm, to just follow him into the shed where they would be out of the wind and snow and could talk. After about ten minutes of work he had the car hooked and pulled free of the snow drift, on the road where it could travel under its own power. He stopped, unhooked the car, put the chains back on the tractor and motioned them to follow him. A few minutes later they were safely inside the shed, shed door closed and out of the snow and wind. The driver climbed out of the car, extended his hand and thanked Bob a few times as they introduced themselves. The man's name was Mark, his wife Mary, and their two boys named James and John, and their daughter named Ruth. After they were all out of the car and the car was shut off, Bob lead them the fifty feet to the back door of the house. Once inside they all breathed a sigh of relief, finally, inside, warm, and safe. Mark explained that they had been trying to get to Bloomington where he was going to try to find work, but in the storm they had gotten off the beaten path and ended up where they were. He said they were down to only about an eighth of a tank of gas and were really getting worried. He said they had been there since about two that afternoon and even with the car running and the heater on it had been getting steadily colder in there.

Bob told them that the storm was expected to continue on into the next day and they would not be able to get out and go anywhere for a while after that since these "back-roads" weren't the top priority for plowing once the storm stopped. Mark and Mary both apologized for ruining their Christmas Eve and asked if there was just a bedroom or something where they could sit and wait out the storm. Martha said she wouldn't hear of it, thought the company on a night like this was a real blessing and they would sit in the family room and get comfortable and do their best to make themselves at home. She had been in the kitchen making soup and cornbread and as the family sat down to watch the weather on the television and try to relax and warm-up, she brought in a big bowl of the soup, a plate of the cornbread and bowls for all five of them. It was obvious they hadn't eaten much for a while as the soup and cornbread all disappeared quickly. Mark and Mary kept apologizing for eating all their food and Martha kept apologizing that all they had was soup. The kids commented that there were no gifts under the tree and Bob explained that Santa hadn't come yet; knowing in his mind that even in the morning when the kids awakened it wouldn't look any different.

The warm house and the warm food in their stomachs had begun to work on the family and within a few minutes Mark and Mary along with all three children were sound asleep on the couch and in the easy chairs. Martha got some blankets and covered all of them and then Bob carried the dishes to the kitchen where they cleaned them and put them away. As they cleaned up Martha turned to Bob with tears running down her cheeks and said, "You know we can't let those kids wake in the morning with nothing under the tree." As she looked at Bob who was agreeing with her she noticed the tears on his cheeks also. Bob spoke softly and said, "You know, Mary is about your size and I have some new tools in the basement that Mark might enjoy and we have some of the better toys left from when the kids were young… what do you think Mrs. Claus, can we give them a Christmas even though we don't have much and they are a long way from anything of their own?"

For the next hour or so Bob and Martha looked through their things, chose, picked over, re-chose, decided and discussed, wrapped and smiled and giggled like kids with their plan. There was a new blouse and slacks for Mary, some new wrenches, screwdrivers, and pliars for Mark, and each of the children had two nice toys wrapped for them, all with their names on them, under the tree. As they turned out the lights, leaving the Christmas tree lights on, and turned to go to their room and go to bed, eager to see how the kids would like it in the morning, Bob thought he saw Mark close his eyes quickly when Bob looked his direction, and he knew he had seen a few tears on his cheeks as he pretended to be still asleep.

The next morning, just barely light outside, still cold, still snowing and blowing, Bob and Martha were awakened by the laughter of small children. Something that old house had missed for the past several years. They dressed quickly and walked out to the living room and the happy, smiling faces of the children and Mark and Mary. The kids had read the names on the presents and knew, yep, Santa had come, as they had been told he would, and they couldn't wait to open the gifts, Mark and Mary were standing behind the children with smiles and tears on their faces and asked Bob what they should do now. Bob laughed and said that Santa had told him years ago that the joy would be better if they had breakfast first then opened the presents, said the extra wait would make it better for the kids. Mark laughed and agreed and the kids moaned their disappointment, wanting to open their gifts. They all moved to the kitchen where Martha had coffee ready and was working on the stove. A few minutes later she brought a bowl of scrambled eggs, plate of toast and some left-over ham to the table. They held hands as Bob said grace and then they did away with the breakfast as quickly as they had the soup and cornbread of the previous evening. Martha laughed and told Mark and Mary that they better get the kids in to see what Santa had brought them. Mary wanted to help clean the kitchen but Martha said she'd do that after they opened the gifts.

Bob gave each of them their gifts and he and Martha stood there smiling as they all opened them, throwing the paper as kids will and playing with the toys. They stood and smiled as the kids and their parents all seemed to enjoy the gifts they had been given. One of the children stopped and looked at Bob and Martha and asked where their gifts were and Bob laughed and said that they must not have been good, Santa had skipped them, and then they turned to go to the kitchen to clean up, but mostly to hide the tears in their eyes as they thought of a child who would think of others and their gifts at a time like this. It didn't take long to clean up the few dishes from breakfast and they were just finishing as they listened to the kids playing when they heard Mark say, "Bob, Tookie, would you come in here please?" Bob wasn't sure what, but he knew something was up as he had not mentioned the name Tookie to their guests and had no idea where Mark had heard that, but they walked into the living room. Mark and Mary were standing in front of the tree, with James, John and Ruth in front of them and they looked different somehow. Mark held an envelope in one hand and a small, beautiful, intricately carved jewelry box in the other. He said, "Bob, you didn't look under the tree very well when you got the gifts earlier, there were two you missed, and they are for you and Martha. You were only interested in what you could do for others and didn't even see that there was something for you. You are both very special people and we wanted to thank you before we left here shortly. The storm hasn't let up a bit but it won't hamper us the way we travel." Bob was handed the envelope. He opened it and it was a title and registration, as well as a set of keys for a brand new pick-up truck. "It is parked out in the shed where you cared enough for us to have us park our car last evening," Mark said. He then handed the beautiful little jewelry box to Martha and said, "Here Tookie, you are most gracious and much loved, and these are for you." Martha opened the small box and it was filled with gold coins and precious stones. "Yes Martha, they are real, and they are for both of you. You had very little but you shared with us. This should help you through the rest of your lives." Then as Bob and Martha watched, the five of them changed from their human forms into their angelic forms, standing before them, shining in their celestial beauty. The one who had been Mark as a human looked at them and said, "For I was an hungered, and ye gave me meat: I was thirsty, and ye gave me drink: I was a stranger and ye took me in: Inasmuch as ye have done it unto one of the least of these my brethren, ye have done it unto me." As they stood there, holding each other, Bob and Martha watched as they faded from sight.

In the next few days Martha noticed that whatever she had been thinking of for supper, when she went to the freezer, it was right there, in the front, waiting for her, and she knew she hadn't bought it while shopping. They noticed that the gifts they had given to the children and Mark and Mary had all been put back in their original location, where they had been before being given to the guests. They have rearranged their living room and moved the Christmas tree into a spot in the corner of the room, and it has become a permanent part of their décor, and they will never forget the greatest Christmas they had in their house.

Be not forgetful to entertain strangers: for thereby some have entertained angels unawares.

www.ingramcontent.com/pod-product-compliance
Lightning Source LLC
Chambersburg PA
CBHW051319120626
46547CB00015B/2308